Reframing the Path to School Leadership

SECOND EDITION

To UNCLE JOE
A decorated WWII Marine Raider
A distinguished educator
Former principal of South Hills High School,
one of America's most innovative campuses
And To
All the other teachers and mentors
Who have helped us along our path.

Reframing the Path to School Leadership

SECOND EDITION

A Guide for Teachers and Principals

LEE G. BOLMAN
TERRENCE E. DEAL

CORWIN
A SAGE Company

For information:

Corwin
A SAGE Company
2455 Teller Road
Thousand Oaks, California 91320
(800) 233-9936
Fax: (800) 417-2466
www.corwin.com

SAGE India Pvt. Ltd.
B 1/I 1 Mohan Cooperative
Industrial Area
Mathura Road,
New Delhi 110 044
India

SAGE Ltd.
1 Oliver's Yard
55 City Road
London EC1Y 1SP
United Kingdom

SAGE Asia-Pacific Pte. Ltd.
33 Pekin Street #02-01
Far East Square
Singapore 048763

Printed in the United States of America

Library of Congress Cataloging-in-Publication Data

Reframing the path to school leadership : a guide for teachers and principals / editors, Lee G. Bolman, Terrence E. Deal. — 2nd ed.
    p. cm.
Earlier ed. entered under: Bolman, Lee G.
Includes bibliographical references.
ISBN 978-1-4129-7819-4 (pbk.)
    1. School management and organization. 2. Educational leadership. 3. Teaching. I. Bolman, Lee G. II. Deal, Terrence E. III. Bolman, Lee G. Reframing the path to school leadership. IV. Title.

LB2805.B58 2010
371.2—dc22   2009053743

This book is printed on acid-free paper.

14   15   16   10   9   8   7   6

Acquisitions Editor: Debra Stollenwerk
Associate Editor: Julie McNall
Editorial Assistant: Allison Scott
Production Editor: Amy Schroller
Copy Editor: Claire Larson
Typesetter: C&M Digitals (P) Ltd.
Proofreader: Wendy Jo Dymond
Cover Designer: Scott Van Atta

Contents

Acknowledgments

This book began as a "portable mentor" for principals, first published in 1993 and joined a year later by a companion guide for teachers. In ensuing years, it became clear to us that we really wanted to write one book for both teachers and principals. That led to the first edition of this book, published in 2002. The ideas in this edition continue to be stimulated by our earlier research on school leadership under the auspices of the National Center for Educational Leadership (NCEL), funded under grants from the U.S. Department of Education. Our friends in Washington, David Stevenson and Ron Anson, were steady sources of both support and constructive criticism, and we remain grateful to both. We also owe much to our colleagues in NCEL for their ideas and encouragement. Ideas from Susan Johnson's work on the school as a workplace, Carol Weiss's work on decision making, and Dan Lortie's studies of the principalship are echoed in this new edition. Reva Chatman's doctoral thesis, "Fresh Roses," a novel about beginning teachers; Tracy Kidder's wonderful chronicle of teacher Chris Zajac in *Among Schoolchildren*; and Frank McCourt's realistic and hopeful portrait of teaching, *Teacher Man,* gave us inspiration and a deeper understanding of classroom life. William Greenfield, Thomas P. Johnson, Ann Lieberman, Gayle Moller, Emmanuel L. Paparella, Roland Barth, and Carrie Sedinger all provided help on earlier versions of the manuscript. Sharon Conley, professor at University of California, Santa Barbara, contributed a dose of support on the final manuscript. Her work on school classified personnel bolstered one of our important premises. Arthur Walton, now the director of the Rochester (NY) Leadership Academy, shared illuminating experiences from his years as a principal and area superintendent in New York City. This new edition benefited greatly from the many helpful suggestions of a constructive and insightful group of teachers, administrators, and scholars who provided critical reviews of the previous edition.

Our spouses, Sandy Deal and Joan Gallos, provided more than the usual support and love—without which writing would be dreary, if not impossible. Each also brought her own special expertise. Sandy Deal's extensive experience as a clinical psychologist greatly strengthened the personal and interpersonal issues in the book. Joan Gallos used her work on gender issues in the classroom and in adult life to provide many helpful insights; Joan's feel for good storytelling also strengthened this work in many ways. Many educators in the United States and abroad have been *our* mentors and guides, and we have learned more from them than we can ever say.

About the Authors

 **Lee G. Bolman** holds the Marion Bloch/Missouri Chair in Leadership at the University of Missouri–Kansas City. An author, teacher, consultant, and speaker, he has written numerous books on leadership and organizations with coauthor Terry Deal, including bestsellers *Leading With Soul: An Uncommon Journey of Spirit* (1995, 2001) and *Reframing Organizations: Artistry, Choice, and Leadership* (1991, 1997), as well as *The Wizard and the Warrior: Leading With Power and Passion* (2006), *The Path to School Leadership* (1993), and *Becoming a Teacher Leader* (1994).

Bolman holds a BA in history and a PhD in organizational behavior from Yale University. He lives in Kansas City, Missouri, with his wife, Joan Gallos, and the youngest of his six children, Bradley.

 **Terrence E. Deal** retired as the Irving R. Melbo Professor at University of Southern California's Rossier School. He is an internationally famous lecturer and author who resides in San Luis Obispo, California, with his wife, Sandy. He has written many books on leadership and organizations. In addition to those written with Lee Bolman, he is the coauthor of *Corporate Cultures* (with Alan Kennedy, 1982), and *Shaping School Culture* (with Kent Peterson, 2008).

Deal received his BA in history from the University of La Verne, his MA from California State University, Los Angeles, and his PhD from Stanford University.

Books by Bolman and Deal have been translated into more than ten languages.

Introduction

If you're a teacher or principal who wants to step up and become a better leader, we wrote this book for you. It's intended as a portable companion, a mentor available anytime you are in need of advice or counsel. You can take it with you, look it over after hours, consult it when trouble arises, and use it to stimulate a reflective dialogue—on your own or with colleagues. The book is filled with the words and wisdom of two seasoned veterans: Margaret Juhl, a master teacher, and Brenda Connors, a wise and warm veteran principal. Though they are fictional characters, they are deeply rooted in the real-world life of contemporary schools. They've been there, and they know what they're talking about because of wisdom gleaned from experience. They are exemplars of countless teachers and principals who are blessed with unusual leadership skills and savvy.

A unique feature of this book is its focus on the intersection between life as a new teacher and the challenges faced by a novice principal. But the lessons are equally relevant for veterans who can profit from looking at their classroom or school in new ways. A second unique feature is spotlighting both teachers *and* principals. They work in the same buildings, but often live in very different worlds and speak dissimilar languages. Absence of mutual understanding and appreciation only exacerbates the inevitable tensions any working relationship will produce. The better each party understands the other's reality, the easier it will be to find mutually acceptable ways of fulfilling the interests of both the school and its students.

Novice teachers and principals, and even those with years of experience, often bounce from one unpleasant shocker to another. Yet the unending torrent of challenges and pitfalls is normal and predictable—if you can interpret the subtle clues. The purpose of this book is to help you decipher what is really going on in schools to avoid the sinking feeling of being caught off guard. The key to becoming a highly effective teacher or principal is to develop powerful habits of mind—profoundly practical ways of thinking about perplexing situations. If they learn them at all, most professionals pick up these lessons painfully in the school of hard knocks—through trial and error. This book offers a quicker, less punishing route to achieving the same end.

Your first challenge as a savvy professional is to figure out the lay of the land. You need a map to make sense of a confusing and messy terrain so that you can master what's really going on and figure out your best options. In diagnosing any situation, you draw on past experience and learning. Both successes and mistakes have fused in mental lenses or windows that you rely on to define and frame reality. Even when your lenses are off target, you're stuck with them, because they're all you've got. Without them, your world would be a senseless blur. For a concrete example, study the following image.

Unless you read Chinese characters, the image makes no sense. If

 you saw it somewhere, perhaps on a menu in a Chinese restaurant, you would probably overlook it. But that's only because you can't decode it. If you could read Chinese, you would recognize it immediately as a very common word. Take another look, and you'll notice that it is composed of two separate characters. Each of these can be a word by itself, and each is a simplified picture of a type of person. Look at the character on the left. What kind of person could it represent? How about the character on the right?

The character on the left is a woman. You can see legs, a body, and a neck. The one on the right is a child. You can see it holding its arms out as if to hug the woman. You might imagine that woman-child together would mean *girl* or *daughter.* But the logic of Chinese script isn't often literal. Together, the two characters form the word *hao,* which means *good.* To the ancient Chinese, and maybe to you as well, portraying a woman and a child together seems pretty positive.

The key point is that if you don't have good mental tools for decoding everyday life in schools, a lot of things might as well be written in Chinese or some other foreign language. Anything that doesn't make sense, you will probably discount or overlook. The trouble is that you'll be ignoring vital signs to help you understand what's going on and what you need to do.

Your prior training in education has provided images to help you become aware of many day-to-day challenges involving individual students, lesson plans, teaching methods, curriculum, budgets, maybe even school law. But you probably received less aid in unraveling the fine points of leadership or in viewing schools as complex systems. University education typically gives short shrift to broadening your vision, sorting out classroom or school social dynamics, or working with others. The primary challenge is transforming schools from the isolating and miserly places they so often become. But the surest route to improvement typically looms as an overwhelming mystery, so our efforts to make things better keep making them worse.

The two of us spend much of our time working with people in so-called "leadership positions"—administrative and managerial roles in organizations worldwide (armies, businesses, hospitals, or governments). The sad truth is that would-be leaders fail more often than they succeed. No one sets out to flunk the leadership test, so why do so many fall short? Most administrators and executives succeed when they can look at things from more than one angle. The best leaders use multiple frames or lenses, each offering a different perspective on common challenges. Framing situations in different ways has many advantages. The most important is the ability to *reframe*. Reframing is a conscious effort to size up a situation from different points of view and then find a novel way to handle it. In times of crisis and overload, you will inevitably feel confused and overwhelmed if you are stuck with only one option. That's the time to go to the balcony and contemplate your alternatives.

Think about dealing with a particularly difficult student or parent. If, as sometimes happens, you get trapped in an inappropriate approach and become immobilized, the student or parent is in control. Other times, you may plunge mindlessly into reckless and misguided action that makes things worse. When we don't know what to do, we do more of what we know—thereby digging ourselves into a deeper hole.

We have identified four frames that are commonly used by principals and teachers in responding to events (Bolman & Deal, 2008):

1. The *political frame* highlights the limits of authority and the reality of scarce resources too limited to fulfill all demands. Schools and classrooms become arenas where individuals and groups jockey for power. Everyone gets caught up in this political vortex. Goals emerge from bargaining and compromise among competing interests rather than from rational analysis. Conflict becomes an inescapable byproduct of everyday life. If handled properly, it can be

a source of constant energy and renewal. If not, schools and classrooms become festering or clashing dog-eat-dog jungles rather than fruitful and harmonious places of learning.

2. The *human resource* frame is often preferred by teachers and principals. It emphasizes individual needs and motives. It sees schools and classrooms much like families that work best when people's needs are satisfied in a caring, trusting environment. Showing concern for others and providing ample opportunities for participation and shared decision making enlist people's commitment and involvement. Many teachers and principals have found that involving others in shaping decisions fosters a sense of ownership.

3. The *structural frame,* prevalent among policy makers and many managers, emphasizes standards and productivity. It assumes that classrooms and schools work best when goals and roles are clear and when diverse efforts are tightly coordinated through authority, policies, and rules. Standards, measures, accountability, and pay for performance are familiar elements of this rational, factory-like approach.

4. The *symbolic frame* focuses attention on culture, meaning, belief, and faith. Like temples or cathedrals, schools and classrooms create symbols to cultivate commitment, hope, and loyalty. Symbols govern behavior through shared values, informal covenants, and unspoken codes. Stories, metaphors, heroes and heroines, rituals, ceremonies, and play add zest and existential buoyancy. The school becomes a joyful way of life rather than a sterile or toxic place of work.

In dealing with leadership challenges, most educators rely primarily on the human resource or structural lenses. Yet many of the situations they face are highly charged politically and emotionally packed symbolically. A school or classroom is a jungle and a cathedral as much as it is a family or a production system. Even young and inexperienced educators need to know how to use power to get things done and how to create symbols to anchor meaning and hope. If you sometimes feel that each day spawns an endless series of ambushes, puzzles, and pitfalls, reframing can help.

In our teaching and consulting, we have presented these ideas to thousands of professionals worldwide. As they learn and apply the frames, they regularly notice the following:

1. The frames help them see things they had overlooked and come to grips with what is really going on.

2. When individuals reframe, they see new possibilities and their responses become more versatile and effective.

This book offers the same lessons to principals and teachers. In a series of intense and intimate dialogues between a newcomer and a seasoned veteran, the novice comes to see situations more clearly, to anticipate trouble in advance, and to develop more successful leadership strategies. Join us for a bumpy, exhilarating ride through a year at Pico School. Meet Joan Hilliard, a new teacher who struggles with predictable challenges. Also get to know her boss, Jaime Rodriguez, a new principal who barely squeaks through his first year. We deliberately made both characters highly committed and talented young professionals who persist in the face of obstacles and are eager to learn from their mistakes. Both are blessed with helpful colleagues (as well as a few daunting opponents). We have all seen plenty of pessimistic accounts of what's wrong with schools. We wanted to provide a view that is both realistic and optimistic—a hopeful image of the possibilities for classroom and school leadership.

OUTLINE OF THE BOOK

At one level, the book is a short novel that tells the story of a year in the life of a school and two newcomers—a new teacher, Joan Hilliard, and a new principal, Jaime Rodriguez. We have tried to make the story an engaging and entertaining read in its own right, but one that carries important lessons about schools and school leadership. To highlight the lessons we have added a primer at the end of each topic. Our larger purpose is to help teachers and principals master the challenges and opportunities of school leadership.

The book is organized into seven parts, each containing one to three chapters and built around a particular topic or theme. Each part concludes with an interlude under the rubric of "Leadership Lessons." Each of the leadership lessons explores key learning points and concludes with a set of reflective questions designed to stimulate both personal reflection and group discussion.

Part I: A Pair of Rookies

Chapter 1, "A New Teacher's First Day," takes Joan Hilliard through her first exciting but troubling day at work. In Chapter 2,

"Getting Off on the Right Foot," Hilliard reflects on her conversation with veteran teacher Margaret Juhl about the disastrous opening faculty meeting with new principal Jaime Rodriguez. As players get to know each other, they go beyond personalities to see new possibilities for building better relationships. Chapter 3, "Newcomers Find Wise Friends and Allies," brings the rookie principal and a wise veteran, Brenda Connors, together. Connors helps Rodriguez sort through the confusing events of his new job to get a better handle on what is happening and what he can do about it.

Part II: The Political Frame

The next two chapters explore a topic that is vital, even though it makes many educators squeamish: school politics. In Chapter 4, "The Old Guard and the New Principal," Rodriguez is dismayed to find that his efforts to take charge and set directions are generating far more conflict and opposition than support or appreciation. In Chapter 5, "The Tracking Wars: School Politics at Work," Hilliard and a group of her colleagues become enthusiastic about building the school's commitment to the district's new inclusion policy. They are disappointed by resistance from other teachers. Margaret talks to Joan about political dynamics in schools and explains how to map them to be more effective.

Part III: The Human Resource Frame

In Chapter 6, "Sagging Morale," rampant dissatisfaction and a vicious, anonymous newsletter alerts Rodriguez to significant morale problems. Brenda Connors guides him through basic human resource frame issues: individual needs, morale, participation, and empowerment.

Part IV: The Structural Frame

Chapter 7, "Student Discipline: Who's Really in Charge?" explores often-neglected issues of school structure. When an effort to revise the discipline policy gets hopelessly bogged down, Connors helps Rodriguez see that the process was unintentionally designed for failure. After clarifying goals, roles, and accountability, the school finally develops a policy that works. Chapter 8, "Standards and

Accountability," looks at the impact of the standards movement and No Child Left Behind in the real world of schools and classrooms.

Part V: The Symbolic Frame

In Chapter 9, "The End of the Year: Symbols and Culture in Schools," Rodriguez wonders why he is still haunted by his predecessor's ghost. Connors helps him understand the symbolic issues of loss and ritual. Key members of the school's informal network develop a powerful and moving transition ceremony, freeing the school to move forward. In Chapter 10, "I'm Just a Great Teacher!" Joan wonders why many of her veteran colleagues have lost the spark and spirit that first brought them to teaching, and laments about years of low pay, lack of respect, and bureaucratic frustrations prevail. At a deeper level, faculty see that they face a crisis of meaning and faith. In developing a celebration of teaching to open the fall term, they create a transforming and reenergizing experience.

Part VI: Values, Ethics, and Spirit

In Chapter 11, "Teaching and Leading: Finding a Balance," the collapse of Joan's relationship with her longtime boyfriend, Larry, becomes the catalyst for a schoolwide discussion about how educators can balance commitments to career, family, and private life.

Chapter 12, "A Talk About Values," explores the role of values in leadership. Rodriguez and Connors discuss the challenges of dealing with dilemmas that arise from ethical conflicts.

Part VII: The Torch Is Passed

Chapter 13, "The Essence of Teaching: Leaving a Legacy," begins when Margaret Juhl is stricken with breast cancer. The entire Pico community rallies. Her bout with mortality leads to a dialogue between Margaret and Joan about the purposes and values underlying the teaching profession. In Chapter 14, "Passing the Torch," Joan Hilliard confronts tragedy and loss, looks deep within herself, and finds the inner strength to rededicate herself to her calling. The story comes full circle as Hilliard and Rodriguez become mentors for another generation of school leaders.

NEW TO THIS EDITION

We think the new edition is stronger in many ways, but most of the changes are subtle, under-the-hood modifications that you might not notice at first glance. The basic story of a new teacher and principal in their first year at Pico School is much as it was. The same cast of characters experiences similar events. But there has been polishing and updating throughout. The most obvious changes are in Chapter 8, "Standards and Accountability." When we wrote the first edition, the No Child Left Behind legislation was still moving through Congress—it was a gleam in reformers' eyes but not yet a reality. Since then, Pico, like schools all over America, has felt the full force of NCLB. Read Chapter 8 to find out how it has played out at Pico.

The Hilliard–Juhl and Rodriguez–Connors dialogues are much like those we have had over the years with fellow educators. Our role is typically to listen and pose questions rather than to provide answers. Inquiry helps people see situations in new ways and recognize promising latent leadership opportunities. When school leaders can reframe events, they become more confident and certain. They feel less anxious and overwhelmed. Most important, they become more effective in getting the right things done.

The book offers a return to an old-fashioned approach to learning a craft. Educators in these pages, even savvy veterans, are far from having all the answers to the mysteries of school leadership. But they are grappling with many of the same questions and issues important to you. We hope you will find yourself identifying and relating their experiences to yours. Only the names change. Even better, you'll be able to think about what you can learn from both their triumphs and their stumbles. In the process, you will probably find fresh ideas and insights to help deal with the age-old challenges you face. We hope that the dialogues will stimulate you to think more deeply about yourself and your leadership. Teachers and principals are among America's most important leaders. Ask a random sample of adults to name the most important leader they have ever known. Many will light up as they remember a caring and gifted teacher or principal who inspired them. Above all, we hope that the book will help you to find new paths to confidence and success, as well as to deepen your dedication to students and others who count on your guidance and inspiration.

PART I

A Pair of Rookies

CHAPTER ONE

A New Teacher's First Day

J oan Hilliard could feel the smile on her face as she stepped from her car. Not the best wheels, but they were hers, a token of four years spent working in a brokerage firm. Joan had always wanted to be a teacher, but she had finished college at the wrong time. To her great disappointment, she couldn't land a teaching position. She had still wanted her own classroom but decided that any job was better than nothing. The brokerage firm paid well, and she felt better for the experience. She had learned about herself, how to work with other adults, and what life at work was all about. Above all, she felt more confident. She had learned to cope in a demanding and stressful adult environment. That experience ought to help in a classroom of kids.

She was delighted to get a teaching assignment at Pico School. It looked like a friendly place from the outside. The surrounding neighborhood was in decline, but Pico boasted green lawns, well-trimmed shrubbery, and large, lattice-paned windows. Built in the 1950s, it had the architectural charm that Joan remembered from the schools of her childhood. As she walked through the arched entryway, she noticed the vaguely familiar smells of new wax and summer mustiness. As she turned down the corridor leading to the principal's office, she ran into a tall, broad-shouldered man with hands on hips, scrutinizing the newly polished sheen on the floor. This had to be the custodian, admiring his work before hundreds of students' feet turned it into a mosaic of scuff marks.

As she moved closer, he looked up and smiled as if he had expected her.

"I'll bet you're Joan Hilliard. Welcome to Pico. I'm Bill Hill, the chief custodian. Let me know if I can help you get settled. I'll stop by occasionally to see how you're doing and let you know what's going on."

"Is this the way to the principal's office?" asked Joan, slightly puzzled about what the custodian might have to offer.

"Straight ahead, second door on the left," Hill replied. "You were a stockbroker, huh? Not as fancy here. You'll have to buy most of your own supplies. Of course, our kids are a lot different from the adults you've been working with. They need a lot of discipline, and a lot of caring, too. My own philosophy is that—"

"Thank you very much, Mr. Hill. I'm sorry I can't chat longer, but I don't want to be late for my meeting with Mr. Rodriguez."

"Oh, don't worry; he's wet behind the ears too. I just hope he's as good as our old principal, Mr. Bailey. We worked together for years. Wonderful man. Anyway, you run along. We'll have plenty of time to talk later. It's good to have a new player on our team."

Joan continued down the hall, all the while trying to make sense out of her encounter with Bill Hill. "You'd think he ran the place. He'll probably read what I put on the board before he erases it. At my old job, the custodians never gave advice on how to forecast the market."

As she opened the glass door labeled "Principal's Office," Joan's reverie was interrupted by a cheerful voice.

"Yoo-hoo, Ms. Hilliard, welcome to Pico!"

The voice belonged to a smiling, gray-haired woman wearing a "Pico Pride" T-shirt over a pair of faded blue jeans.

"I'm Phyllis Gleason, the school secretary. Mr. Rodriguez was called to the superintendent's office unexpectedly. He'll fill you in on the school and your assignment when he gets back. In the meantime, he asked me to show you around. Would you like a cup of coffee before we start?"

"Sure, why not?"

As Phyllis went off in search of coffee, the door to an office marked "Assistant Principal" opened, and a short, square-shouldered, graying man walked out. He looked at Joan, frowned, and asked, "Who are you?"

His tone and crew cut reminded Joan of a grizzled Marine drill sergeant. She was surprised at how nervous she felt. "Oh, uh, I'm sorry. I'm Joan Hilliard, and I—"

"Oh, yeah!" the man interrupted, with the commanding tone of someone who expected to be listened to. "I heard about you. No teaching experience. Just what we need. You sure as hell didn't learn anything about classroom control from a bunch of stockbrokers. Most of them don't even know anything about the market, much less about handling kids."

With that, he marched forcefully out of the office just as Phyllis returned with the coffee.

Joan must have looked as crestfallen as she felt, because Phyllis seemed to understand immediately what had happened.

"Oh goodness, you met Mr. Shepherd."

"I didn't exactly meet him," Joan replied. "He didn't bother to tell me who he is. Is he always so, um . . . " Joan paused, looking for a discreet way to phrase her question.

"Gruff? Oh, don't take it personally. His bark is worse than his bite. He's the same with everyone."

"He's the assistant principal?"

"Yes, been here ten years. Some people thought he might be the next principal. But the superintendent felt that Mr. Shepherd should do what he does best. He's *awfully* strong on discipline."

Did Phyllis intend praise or veiled criticism of the assistant principal? Joan decided not to press the issue. Would the principal be as abrupt as Sam Shepherd? Why was the secretary taking charge of her orientation? As Phyllis started to lead her around the building, Joan wondered if the tour would simply fill some time. But her doubts gradually turned to awe and admiration. Phyllis seemed to know all and share most in loving detail, as if she had witnessed everything firsthand. With unflagging enthusiasm, Gleason introduced Joan to everyone they encountered, and Joan was impressed with the warmth of the responses. Joan was even more amazed by Gleason's ability to field questions on just about everything—schedules, materials, children, parents—you name it.

They treat her like the school oracle—knows all, broadcasts the good stuff. Whatever she says is the way it is, thought Joan to herself. Maybe Phyllis really runs the school.

It was only as they neared the end of the tour that Joan realized how much she had shared of her own background and ideas about teaching.

She seems as interested in my thoughts about teaching as Bill Hill, the custodian, did, mused Joan.

Phyllis stopped in front of a door with a translucent window marked "208." She took Joan inside a spacious, sun-filled classroom and said, "This is your room this year. What do you think? Maybe it's a little plain compared to what you're used to. But within these four walls, you're the boss."

"It's great! Lots of windows and plenty of wall space and bookshelves. The walls are a little bare, but we'll take care of that in no time."

Joan's mind was flooded with a thousand thoughts. She tried to imagine the empty desks filled with students. Her students. Her classroom. She'd waited a long time for this.

Phyllis paused for a few moments while Joan took it all in. "I'll leave you alone for a while to think about what else you'll need. Whatever it is—supplies, good advice, breaking news—I'll try to get it for you."

"Thanks, Phyllis," said Joan. Then a question occurred to her. "Who had this room before me?"

"Oh, well, *him*," Phyllis replied. "He didn't stay long. Nice young man. Smart, too. But he had trouble with discipline. The noise and the fights were the biggest problem. It *was* entertaining to walk by his classroom. Never a dull moment. But don't let that worry you. I'm sure you'll be different. Just remember not to smile before December. And anything you need to know, come to me."

Phyllis smiled once again and started back to the office. She turned her head only to let Joan know that the new principal had returned and wanted to see her.

All Joan knew about the new principal was his name: Jaime Rodriguez. At first glance, the dark suit and trim moustache looked right, but he seemed shyer and more boyish than she'd expected.

Is he old enough to be a principal? she wondered. But his greeting was warm and cordial. Their conversation flowed easily, and they seemed to think a lot alike.

What she didn't know at the time was that, even as they talked, Jaime was thinking back to his first day as principal only a few weeks earlier. He'd arrived eager to apply all he'd learned in his master's program at State University. But he soon realized that it was going to be harder than he imagined. Why wasn't there a reserved parking space for the principal? Then as he walked up to the main entrance he ran into Bill Hill, who was pruning the shrubbery. After a brief greeting, Jaime asked, "Aren't you cutting those a little short?"

Hill's retort, "Mr. Bailey likes them that way," seemed brusque.

Who's the principal, me or Bailey? Jaime wondered. Being the boss might not be as easy as he assumed.

His first encounter with Phyllis Gleason reinforced his concern. On the surface, she seemed pleasant enough. But behind the warmth,

Jaime sensed an undertone of resentment. He was caught off guard by the story of the desk. The principal's office was dwarfed by a huge oak desk, and Phyllis regaled him with the story of how Mr. Bailey had made it himself from an old oak tree toppled by a tornado.

"He's a wonderful man and the best boss a person could have."

Her use of the present tense was another reminder to Jaime that, even if he had the title, he still had to earn the principal's job. He was delighted to see Joan as a possible ally. She was new too, and her philosophy of education seemed almost identical to his.

After her rescheduled meeting with Jaime, Joan mulled over her morning's encounters. Nothing was quite as she expected. Why did the secretary and the custodian loom so large in the affairs of the school? How many people would be looking over her shoulder and giving her advice on how to teach? She had almost raised her concerns with Jaime, but thought better of it. He seemed friendly and genuinely pleased that she was joining the Pico faculty, but she didn't want to sound like an idiot. Still, the two had formed an almost instant bond as they realized what they shared—both were new and nervous. Joan could hardly believe her luck in finding a principal who seemed so supportive and easy to work with.

The day's thoughts were still spinning in Joan's mind as she walked to her car for the drive home. Just as she was opening the car door, she heard someone calling her name. She turned her head and saw a group of people chatting in the parking lot. One of them, a man who fit Joan's stereotype of a veteran football coach past his peak, came over.

"Joan Hilliard?" he said as he walked over and offered his hand. "I'm Phil Leckney. My classroom is just down the hall from yours. Welcome to Pico. Some of us are headed over to Andy's Café. Would you like to join us?"

Joan felt torn. She didn't want to alienate her new colleagues before she'd even met them, but she'd promised to meet her boyfriend, Larry, in half an hour. After hesitating, she replied, "Well, I can stay for only a little while, but I'd love to."

The conversation at Andy's reinforced Joan's feeling that she had come to the right school. Her new colleagues laughed heartily when she told of her encounters with Bill Hill and Phyllis Gleason.

"To understand Bill," Margaret Juhl responded, "come in some morning at 7:30 and go to the cafeteria. You'll see the free breakfast kids. And you'll see that Bill is a big brother for just about everyone in the room. He knows all the students and a lot of the parents too.

Bill grew up a few blocks from here. He probably knows more people in the neighborhood than anyone else at Pico."

"Well, it might be a draw between him and Phyllis," Phil Leckney chimed in.

"True," said Margaret. "She's sort of a combination of Dear Abby, Katie Couric, and General Patton. The key thing to remember is the line from the old song, 'You can get anything you want, at Phyllis's restaurant.'"

Joan joined everyone else's laughter. As the group quieted down, Joan was caught off guard by a question from Vivian Chu.

Vivian, another veteran, had not said much until she turned to Joan to ask, "You met with Mr. Rodriguez today, didn't you? How did it go?"

Joan felt every eye at the table turn to her. It dawned on her that her colleagues were as curious as she was about Pico's new principal.

As Phil put it, "He's an unknown. Phil Bailey was a great guy. Not Mr. Super Principal, maybe, but he was supportive, and he left us alone to teach. New principals are all alike. They want to save the world and change everything. They don't understand the idea, if it ain't broke, don't fix it. How hard will it be to break this guy in?"

No one seemed to know the answer. The consensus was that they would learn a lot more the next day at the opening faculty meeting of the new school year. Then the conversation shifted to Joan's experience in the business world. Her colleagues peppered her with questions about what she did, what it was like, and, to her embarrassment, how much money she made. It almost felt as if they wished they had tasted another career themselves to find out if the grass was greener somewhere else. The conversation at Andy's was so engrossing that Joan was startled to look at her watch and notice that she was a half hour late to meet Larry. Bidding her colleagues a hasty farewell, she rushed off. On balance, she felt, it had been a great day. But she knew Larry didn't like waiting. She just hoped he wouldn't be too miffed.

CHAPTER TWO

Getting Off on the Right Foot

"So, when are you done today?"

Joan heard the edge in Larry's voice. He was still in bed, and she was putting the final touches on her teaching attire.

"I'm not sure, Larry," she said carefully. "Margaret and I are meeting with the principal to talk about his opening sermon. You remember, I told you about it."

"Oh, yeah. Rodriguez did his vision thing, and Margaret cut him off at the knees."

"Well, not quite," said Joan, as she thought back a few days to the year's first faculty meeting. She had entered the gathering with optimism and excitement. She knew that Jaime wanted to get off on the right foot as much as she did. After a few preliminaries, he began to speak about his vision for the school. Joan felt excited by his image of a child-centered school in which all students were expected to achieve at their full potential. In her previous job, there never seemed to be any real sense of mission beyond making money.

Rodriguez had seemed tense, but he delivered his message with conviction, even fervor. Joan soon realized, however, that the audience wasn't buying. Some teachers looked bored. Others appeared openly resistant. A few rows behind her, she could hear Phil Leckney making snide comments to those nearby.

When Jaime finished, he asked for questions. At first, none came. The silence was oppressive. When had she had felt more tension in a room? The stony silence broke only when Margaret Juhl asked, "Shouldn't you get to know this school and how we do things before you preach about how we should teach?"

Joan was startled by Margaret's bluntness and felt pained when she glanced at Jaime. He looked stunned, almost frozen in place. Joan wished she had the courage to go over and give him a hug.

He looks like he needs help, she thought to herself in the seconds before another young teacher, Carlos Cortez, leaped to his feet. His anger felt like a slap.

"The man just got here and you people don't want to give him a chance. Mr. Rodriguez is saying things someone has needed to say for a long time. I'm getting pretty tired of people who think this school is so perfect that we can't improve."

Cortez's outburst triggered a series of sharply worded exchanges between older and younger teachers.

What did I get myself into? Joan began to wonder. The brokerage was never like this. It was competitive, even ruthless, but people never went for the jugular.

She was relieved when Rodriguez moved to adjourn the meeting.

After the meeting, Joan asked Margaret to explain what had happened.

"Well," she said, "I'm still sorting it out myself. Jaime is probably feeling a little shell-shocked, wondering what hit him. I'm probably not his favorite teacher right now.

"Aren't you worried about that?"

"Only if he stays angry. He could make life harder for me if he wanted to."

"Do you think maybe you should apologize, or something?"

"Of course not. He may not know it yet," said Margaret with a smile, "but I was doing him a favor."

"That was a favor?" Joan asked incredulously.

"You were there. You saw all those stony faces. He meant well, but his speech flopped. He didn't have a clue about what was going wrong. It may take a little while, but I hope he'll realize that I was telling him what he needed to hear—why the teachers didn't like his opening salvo."

"But, what if he doesn't listen?"

"We'll know soon. He called me and asked for a meeting."

"And what about Carlos?" Joan looked worried.

"I'll talk to Carlos. I don't want him to think I'm out to get our first Latino principal. The truth is I want Jaime to succeed as much as Carlos does. If you really want to torpedo an administrator, you don't do it head on. You kill them softly behind the scenes. It's safer and works better. You may have seen it in your last job. Rodriguez was digging himself into a hole. Someone had to tell him. And remind him about the first law of holes."

"The first law of holes?"

"When you're in one, stop digging!" said Margaret with a laugh. "Anyway, if I talk to Carlos one-on-one about how we can help the new principal succeed, I think we can have a meeting of the minds."

"I don't know," said Joan skeptically. "He seemed pretty upset."

"Joan, when I was younger, I used to pussyfoot around conflict. As a little girl, I heard all the messages about being nice and not upsetting anyone. But I've learned since that you don't do any favors by holding back and keeping people in the dark."

"I heard those same messages. It's still hard for me to deal with all the tension and hurt feelings."

"Me, too. But teaching is not an exact science. We're not always going to agree with one another. When we're at odds on things we care about, how in the world can we talk about disagreements without having anyone feel anything?"

"Maybe that's why everyone's trying to ignore the tensions between the Latino and Anglo teachers?"

"Exactly. People are hoping that if we ignore it, it will go away. But we know it won't. In the meantime, we hurt the kids as much as we hurt each other. It's the same with the other conflicts we try to brush aside. They pile up and then blow up. That's not my idea of a healthy school. How can you deal with anything if you can't talk about it? In the long run, it's more productive to get things out in the open."

"Maybe. But you really left Jaime hanging. He looked crushed."

"I know—it was painful for both of us. But the one thing worse than hearing something straight is never hearing anything at all. There were a lot of unhappy teachers in that room. If that stays hidden, teachers think their new principal is a jerk, but he won't know it. Down the road, teachers will drag their feet on everything he's doing. We'll think he's a tyrant, and he'll think we're dinosaurs."

"So everyone blames someone else, and the school gets stuck. But why did you convene a meeting at Andy's Café without Jaime? Weren't you being less than open yourself?"

"Teachers needed to talk about what happened. When I spoke up, I was speaking for a lot of other people. You remember the conversation at Andy's?"

"Hard to forget. Venting, criticism, anger. But after a while, the tone started to shift. You could see some teachers almost starting to feel sympathy for Jaime."

"Exactly."

"Were you nudging the conversation in that direction?"

Margaret smiled broadly. "Sure I was. I could do that because people trust me. They saw me stand up to Jaime, and I've stood up for teachers before. By the end of the evening, people were a little more willing to give him another chance. That's what I hoped for."

"But I still feel bad for him. He's new like me. It's bad enough that my boyfriend criticizes everything I cook. The first few days with my class, I've done more things wrong than right. I don't know if I could handle being picked apart like that."

Margaret's face softened. Her voice was warm and gentle. "I know. Jaime may feel the same way. I remember how much support I needed as a new teacher. But I also needed someone to level with me when I was screwing up. Do you want to keep feeding Larry stuff he hates? If I have suggestions for your teaching, do you want me to keep them to myself?"

"If it helps me teach better, maybe I could even tolerate public humiliation. But I'd still feel lousy. Jaime is pretty upset."

"Sure he is. Building a relationship takes more than hit and run. I have to follow up. That's next."

As Joan wound down her thoughts about her previous conversation with Margaret, she took her last sip of coffee.

Larry interrupted her reverie. "Earth to Joan! Earth to Joan! You've been staring at the coffeepot for the last five minutes. I thought you were bringing me a cup."

"I'm sorry, honey. I guess I was still thinking about the school. Anyway, I'm sure the meeting today can't last beyond five o'clock. How about pizza? My treat?"

"Sounds great, but only if the pizza isn't topped with pepperoni *and* Pico."

"I promise," said Joan laughing.

There were still moments when Larry was as delightful as she remembered him in graduate school. But he had seemed more supportive of her career when they were both in the same business. Now that she was teaching, he seemed to expect that *her* workday should last from the time *he* left in the morning until *he* got home at night. Joan couldn't help wondering if they would make it over the long haul.

CHAPTER THREE

Newcomers Find Wise Friends and Allies

As Jaime Rodriguez looked from his office into the empty school yard, he mulled over his first days as principal of Pico. It had been a lot rockier than he'd expected. In his first presentation, he'd hoped to impress the faculty with his dedication and vision. He'd missed the mark by a wide margin. After the meeting, things continued to spiral downward. He was grateful for one thing. Just when he was going under for the third time, he'd found someone who would become his coach—Brenda Connors, a veteran principal in a neighboring school. Jaime bumped into her as they were leaving a meeting at the county office.

"How's it going at Pico?" Brenda asked.

Jaime hesitated, wondering if she really wanted to know. But she'd impressed him in the meeting. She seemed to be the kind of principal he hoped to become: caring, confident, and professional.

Avoiding the temptation to give a pat answer, he asked, "Do you want the truth?"

"Nothing but."

Jaime hesitated, but finally decided to plunge in. "If I didn't have a new house and a big mortgage, I might pack it in."

Connors's response was warm and direct. "That's about how I felt. Almost twenty years ago, but still seems like yesterday. How about a cup of coffee?"

"How about something a little stronger?"

"I think I know just the place,"

Once they found a comfortable table and ordered drinks, Brenda opened the conversation.

"I asked how things were going because I still remember my first week on the job. I was thinking no one could be as scared and confused and still make it. Everything was blowing up in my face. Angry teachers. School in chaos. I was feeling pretty hopeless. But then I got a break I wasn't expecting.

"The assistant superintendent then was a grizzled old character named Harold Sawyer. Everyone called him 'Buzz.' He was a couple of years from retirement. He scared me at first. He seemed so demanding and impatient. I was afraid he couldn't believe that they'd tried to make a principal out of someone with so little talent. At the end of the first week, he dropped by my office. I froze. I was afraid he'd come to tell me to pack up my desk and get out before I did any more damage. I was petrified. But I'll never forget his words. 'You know,' he said rather nostalgically, 'this used to be my office. I was principal here for twelve years. The first couple, I didn't have a clue about what in hell I was doing. If the staff hadn't carried me along, the parents would have ridden me out of town on a rail. You'll probably learn quicker than I did. But being a new principal is a lot like flying in a fog with no radar. If you're interested in making your way, I could give you a few tips.'

"I'd have hugged that man except I was too afraid of what he might think. It turned out he meant what he said. He was the life preserver that got me through the first year. He became more than a tutor. He was one of my best friends. Even after he retired, we kept in touch"—she paused and lowered her head—"until he died a couple of years ago."

Jaime thought he saw a trace of tears in her eyes.

"I miss him. Anyway, Jaime, if you'd like someone to talk with, I'm volunteering."

"I can sure use the help. But it's hard to believe your first year was that rough."

Brenda smiled. "In a few years, some young principal will tell you the same thing."

Jaime mulled over that first conversation with a smile. Brenda's warmth and insights had been more valuable than the drink. She encouraged him as he tried to explain why his first days had been so unsettling. What surprised him most was that she could make sense of things he couldn't figure out.

When he started at Pico, Rodriguez planned to take charge and set high standards for both staff and students. He was counting on his interpersonal skills to win people over. He'd always been good at building relationships, even with those who saw things differently. He felt he could do the job at least as well as other principals he had known. Above all, he felt excited about the contribution he hoped to make. Schools were under fire from all quarters, and Jaime wanted Pico to set an example of what was possible.

But that was before his now-infamous first faculty meeting. He painfully recalled the details. When he had entered the meeting room minutes before the official starting time, he was disappointed to find no one there. His discouragement grew as teachers slowly drifted in. He was particularly offended by some who registered hopes that the meeting wouldn't last very long.

He opened the meeting by talking about his vision. He'd done his homework—hours of it. He shared his dreams of a child-centered school that set high standards for all students. But as he talked, he noticed teachers frowning or crossing their arms. Some were staring out the window or at papers in front of them. After he finished, he asked for questions. A long silence ensued. Then Margaret Juhl hit him with her question about telling them how to teach before he knew them. Jamie was stunned, like he'd been punched in the gut. He'd hoped to fire them up. Maybe he had—but not the way he wanted. It had never occurred to him to have a Plan B. He was caught flat-footed. Before he regained his balance, a small war broke out between his critics and defenders. Fearing things were getting out of hand, he'd moved quickly to adjourn the meeting. He left feeling like a failure.

The next morning was no better. As he was walking to his office, he ran into Bill Hill.

"Heard you gave a speech," said Bill.

"What did you hear?"

"Well . . ." Bill hesitated for a moment, as if trying to gauge the principal's reaction. "Folks say you can talk the talk. But they wonder if you really know what you're doing and can walk the walk."

Rodriguez stared at Hill blankly for a moment before stammering, "Thanks." He fled to his office in search of a quiet refuge, but the phone was ringing as he walked in. It was his first call from Mildred Hofsteder, the superintendent of schools.

"Jaime," she said, "You've got good ideas—raising standards, a child-centered school. I'm one hundred percent behind you. But you can't get much done if the faculty isn't with you."

When it rains, it pours, Jaime thought to himself. How did word get around so fast? What's going on here?

Only later did he learn about the informal gathering, Margaret Juhl presiding, at Andy's Café following the faculty meeting. It was clear he had been left off the guest list. Jaime knew Margaret was a twenty-two-year veteran of the Pico faculty. He'd heard that most of the senior teachers respected her, and many parents revered her. She had also served for a number of years as the representative of the teachers union.

He knew he'd gotten off on the wrong foot. But where had he gone wrong? His discomfort increased over the next several days with a steady stream of teacher comments about the merits of his predecessor, Phil Bailey. Jaime got tired of hearing, "That's not how Mr. Bailey would have done it." Was Bailey's ghost running the school?

As he poured all this out in the first conversation with Brenda, she listened attentively, occasionally offering a comment or question. The more they talked, the better Jaime felt. Brenda could see things in ways that he couldn't. She helped him recognize the difference between having a title and gaining the respect of the teachers. She explained that new leaders always undergo some form of initiation ritual or "hazing." She reminded him that people need time to adapt to change and reassured him that comparisons to Phil Bailey were a normal part of transition, not a sign that Jaime would never be accepted.

Jaime remembered asking Brenda at the end of their conversation if they could meet again. "Principals need to stick together, and I got a lot of help when I was new," she had replied. "I owe it to Buzz to return the favor. Besides, I enjoy our time together."

That night, Jaime slept better than he had in weeks.

While Jaime passed the night peacefully, Joan Hilliard was pacing the floors of her small apartment. She had repeated over and over, "I've lost them. My classroom is a zoo. A mob of predators all trying to hunt down the same prey . . . me."

She tried to pinpoint where she had gone wrong. She was excited about teaching and her philosophy seemed to dovetail with the principal's. But her students had different priorities: Making mischief seemed to top their lists. Learning was only a distant annoyance.

She recalled Phyllis Gleason's passing reference to her predecessor's demise: "He was a good teacher but couldn't control a class."

That's me, she thought, a one-year wonder. Great enthusiasm but no clue on how to manage a bunch of energetic kids. What's worse is that I don't know where to turn for help. I sink or swim on my own, and right now I'm going down fast.

Two days later, Joan sat at her desk, her face buried in crossed arms. It had been the day from hell. Her little nemesis, Roscoe, had been on a tear with Armando, his partner in making trouble. Together, they enlisted their classmates into their destructive frolic. Even Heidi, her top student, joined the bedlam. At the low point in her depressed soliloquy, she heard a familiar voice at her classroom door: "Tough day?"

Margaret came in and sat across from Joan. "We've all had them. My first years were horrific. I thought about quitting almost every day. I'm not sure why I stayed. I was stubborn, I guess, and didn't have anything better to do."

"But you're the best teacher at Pico," Joan protested.

"Not then. After a couple of years, the light bulb lit up: I wasn't teaching my kids. I was only thinking about the content I was trying to stuff into their heads. But I didn't know them. When I was studying to be a teacher, we learned lesson plans and teaching strategies, but we didn't think much about what kids need or the dynamics of a classroom. You know one thing that really did help? I took a course in organizational behavior. I learned that schools are a lot like businesses. Human dynamics rule the roost. Classrooms are the same—only in miniature. I started to rethink what it means to be a teacher. I'd been thinking of myself as a fount of knowledge, pouring content into empty minds. Content is part of the job, but I realized I also needed to be a classroom manager and leader."

"Classroom manager and leader" echoed in Joan's mind as she drove home. "Whatever that means, I'm not doing it. But I need to learn fast."

LEADERSHIP LESSONS I

Seeing and Solving Entry Barriers

Starting a new job or a new career is one of life's great moments. The road ahead promises adventure, opportunity, and independence. Long-delayed dreams can finally be realized. Everything seems possible. Bumps? Obstacles? Who wants to think about such things when the world is alive with possibilities? Yet in a fresh situation filled with opportunities, there are always land mines concealed just below the surface. Too often, we discover them only when they blow up in our faces. Enthusiasm and optimism can quickly erode into a mire of disappointment and disillusionment.

Newcomers will always encounter bumps on an unfamiliar road. Joan's and Jaime's experiences offer guidelines for spotting and avoiding pitfalls with minimal wear and tear. They were luckier than many other neophytes because they found wise guides and allies experienced in managing and leading in the perplexing and fiery world of schooling. Direct encounters in that crucible forge lessons that can be passed along. Year after year, thousands of eager new teachers and principals like Joan and Jaime arrive brimming with enthusiasm and idealistic visions, only to learn that their skills and understanding fall well short of what it takes to deal with hard and stubborn realities. Wise friends and mentors are vital for getting off on the right foot—or correcting missteps.

Expect to Be Tested

When you enter a new situation, you're busy trying to find your way and make a good first impression, while the natives are actively trying to size you up. Will you fit in? Might you be a troublemaker? A threat? Joan was put under a microscope multiple times in her first few hours at Pico. The custodian, Bill Hill, tested her flexibility and receptivity when he told her he'd be stopping by to see how she was doing. Sam Shepherd, the assistant principal, tested her resilience and self-confidence with his challenging and chilly greeting. Later, her students provided a baptism of fire that nearly did her in. Joan could easily have responded in ways that caused her new colleagues to see her as difficult and rigid or, conversely, as weak and easy to manipulate. Pay attention to these encounters. They are important clues about people's expectations and about yardsticks they use to evaluate one another. Scoping out the new situation is just as important as trying to make a good first impression.

Pay Attention to Subtle Clues and Signs

As soon as Joan walked into Pico, she began to pick up clues about how the school actually worked. Many were surprises. Joan wisely paid attention to what she was finding—and tried not to take too much for granted. But her inexperience made it hard for her to anticipate the next challenge and to know what to do when it arrived, as when her students first tested her authority and mettle.

When you walk through any school, it will begin to reveal its secrets and ways. What do you first notice when you enter the building? How does the place look? How does it smell? Joan noticed the clean floors, the smell of fresh wax, and the custodian appraising his work. What sounds, if any, stand out? Walk around to get a wider view. Notice artifacts—banners, photos, trophy cases. Is there a sign that says "Welcome"? Or merely one that says "All visitors must report immediately to the principal's office"? What's on the walls? Photos of students? Random graffiti? Notice what people wear. Is the principal in a dark suit? Or an aloha shirt? Pay particular attention to how people greet you. Joan's frosty encounter with the assistant principal was offset by warmer welcomes from Bill Hill and Phyllis Gleason.

If you pay attention, your observations will yield many clues to penetrate a fog-shrouded new situation. But there's more you can do. Finding your way around is a lot easier if you get help from local guides.

Identify Informal Guides:
Mentors, Priests, and Storytellers

There's a cast of characters in every workplace who can be recruited as mentors and guides. Locate informal priests or priestesses. You won't always find them in a big corner office. They may be typing away in a small cubicle, like Phyllis Gleason, or polishing floors, like Bill Hill. They're often old-timers who came in with the furniture. They can tell you how things came to be and instruct you in cultural mores and norms. Be reverent, pay attention, and you'll discover a storehouse of knowledge and wisdom. You can also make friends whose counsel and support may be a lifesaver down the line.

Look, too, for storytellers—individuals like Phyllis who dramatize everyday exploits and perpetuate school lore. Listen to their tales and read between the lines. Joan learned more than she expected as Phyllis led a guided tour of the school building. Along the way, Gleason's casual comment about Joan's predecessor, who couldn't control his class, was a gentle warning about possible trouble ahead.

If you listen and keep your eyes open, you'll acquire important lessons on what works and what to avoid. Informal sources can tell you things you'd almost never find in policy manuals. Stories make these important lessons real and memorable. Even though unofficial, the messages are often right on. Stories also recount the memorable deeds of heroes and heroines—living logos who exemplify what the organization stands for. Phil Bailey, the former principal, Brenda Connors, the veteran principal, and Margaret Juhl, the master teacher, all typify this classic role.

On the other hand, you might find that the heroes are folks who toe the line and kiss up, or cynics who complain all the time and run the school down. If that's what gets rewarded, but it's not your style, you've learned an important lesson. Maybe you're just the positive force this school needs, or maybe this isn't the place for you. In the latter case, it's better to move along and search for a better fit.

Connect With the Grapevine

Gossips are always privy to the latest scoop—even things that are supposed to be confidential or hush-hush. Hear them out, and you'll often get the best briefing available. Their accuracy isn't always perfect, but they're usually fairly reliable indicators of what's really going on. If you hear a story about the principal getting chewed out by the superintendent in a private hallway conversation, the details may be distorted, but you can trust that something is afoot. Rumors of impending layoffs may be exaggerated, but you'd be wise to prepare for rough seas. Gossip is a two-way street. You have to give in order to receive. You can overdo it by revealing confidences or giving people the impression that you're a backbiter and nothing is safe with you. But don't be too cautious about divulging a few things yourself. Chances are the truth will be less harmful than what the gossips make up on their own. A few minutes over coffee with your local gossip is often worth more than a multitude of meetings and memos. Information is power. Being up to date and in the loop gives you a real advantage over people who rely solely on the official channels to keep on top of things. If there are things you'd like people to be talking about, there's no better vehicle than the grapevine to get the word out.

Reflective Questions

1. When you entered your current school, what kind of tests or initiation rituals did you encounter? What impact did they have on you? What did you learn from them?

2. If you're a veteran at your school, how does the school initiate newcomers? Does it do a good or bad job of helping them fit in and learn their way around?

3. How would you describe the culture of your school? What are the most important icons, rituals, stories, and ceremonies? Can you identify heroes, villains, priests, or storytellers? Is the culture widely shared or splintered? In what ways does the culture help or hurt the school's ability to achieve its educational mission?

4. Is there an active grapevine in your school? Do you participate? What kind of information moves on the grapevine? What is the impact on the school?

5. As you took the reins of your new assignment, were you formally hooked up with a mentor or coach? If not, did someone informally offer advice and support? Is there a trusted veteran who might show you the ropes if asked? How might you best approach this person for some advice or assistance?

PART II

The Political Frame

CHAPTER FOUR

The Old Guard and the New Principal

The morning after his meeting with Brenda Connors, Rodriguez found himself mulling over their conversation. He particularly remembered her advice about the political realities of schools. At first, he had protested.

"I don't want politics to govern my school. I've seen what it can do—endless squabbling, behind-the-scenes plots, everyone pursuing some parochial interest. I'm an educator, not a politician. My hero is John Dewey, not Machiavelli. Politics 101 was not part of our university curriculum—for a reason."

Connors had not challenged him directly. She simply asked, "What do you make of the superintendent's phone call?"

"It's a puzzle. I've got some clues, but I don't know how to put them together."

"Let's start with who might have a pipeline to the superintendent."

"Beats me. I wish I knew."

"Well, let's try to scope out Pico's political terrain. Who are the influential people who might not be thrilled with your arrival?"

Jaime was embarrassed to realize that he had not thought much about potential opposition. He paused before responding.

"Well, there's Sam Shepherd, the assistant principal. He was passed over for my position. He still thinks he's the right man for the job. He knows how to crack the whip, but he's more like a warden than a leader. Most of the black and Latino parents feel he doesn't respect them or their kids."

"Who else?" Brenda asked.

"There's Margaret Juhl. She's a veteran. Teachers and parents respect her. She nailed me at the first faculty meeting. After I talked about my vision for the school, she pretty much told me I had no right to tell teachers how to teach. It felt like a slap in the face. The room got very tense."

Brenda nodded understandingly. "I know Margaret. She definitely has a mind of her own, and she's not shy about telling you what's on it. But she's a pro. Spend some time with her. She could be an asset and an ally."

Jaime groaned. "Do you think I'm a glutton for pain?"

Brenda smiled. "No. But Margaret's a very important player. Do you know what Lyndon Johnson said about people like that?"

"No, what?"

"It's a lot better to have them inside the tent peeing out, than outside the tent peeing in."

They both laughed.

"OK, I've got your point. I'll talk to Margaret."

Then she asked, "So far, you've focused on the professional staff. Are there other influential players?"

Jaime thought for a minute. "There's Bill Hill, the custodian. People say he's the eyes and ears of the school and the community. Seems to know just about everything that goes on both inside and outside Pico. And he's not bashful about sharing it. Then there's the secretary, Phyllis Gleason. She probably knows more than I'll ever know about Pico. She knows the times past and where all the bodies are buried. I really need her. But I don't get the feeling she's delighted having me as her new boss."

He stopped and frowned. "The more I think about it, the worse it seems. I'm new. I got off on the wrong foot. And I have a lot of opposition."

"Who are your allies?"

Jaime hesitated for a moment. "Beats me."

"What about your younger staff?"

"Well, some of them are pretty frustrated. They think the school's too conservative, that it doesn't really respond to kids. There are three Latino teachers in the school, and I know they were glad to see me get the job. One of them, Carlos Cortez, came to my defense after Margaret ambushed me. He tells me that the Latino teachers resented Phil Bailey for never doing anything to celebrate Cinco de Mayo or observe other Latino traditions."

"What's your relationship like so far with Phyllis?" Brenda inquired.

"As I said, I think she's still comparing me to Phil," Jaime responded, "but the assistant superintendent says that she loves the school and is absolutely loyal."

"Talk to Phyllis and Bill Hill. When you're in a fog, you need some navigational clues. They might be able to help you get a better fix on what's going on. And what you might need to do next."

"What do you mean?"

"One of the things they never teach in graduate school is how to map the political terrain. My first year as a principal, we had *big* budget cuts. Talk about a jungle! When there's a drought and the watering hole starts to dry up, the animals get desperate trying to protect their turf. Survival and brute force are the order of the day. I realized right away that I had to figure out who the key players were, what they wanted, and how much power they had. I decided to approach the issue systematically since so much was at stake. I nosed around, talked to some people and asked questions. Then, I actually drew a map on a piece of paper. On the right side, I put the real conservatives, the people who were probably going to resist almost any change I came up with. On the left, I put those who I was pretty sure I could count on. Then, in the middle, I put fence-sitters who might go either way. There were a lot of them, and that told me something right away."

"You needed those swing voters?"

"Exactly. As I put folks on the map, I positioned them higher or lower, depending on how much power I believed they had. Then I thought about how we could negotiate, instead of going to war. When a new principal comes in, all the old issues get opened up. Interest groups jockey to hold on to what they have and see if they can get more."

Jaime felt uncomfortable with all the talk of power and politics. But Brenda made sense.

"So you're saying I need to figure out who's with me and who's against me. Essentially, I need to draw my own map." He had the look of someone reluctantly accepting a new idea. Then he got it: "I think I'll talk to Phyllis and Bill tomorrow."

While shaving the next morning, Rodriguez found himself reassessing his situation. Before arriving at Pico, he had images of leading a motivated and harmonious faculty who were delighted with their new principal. Seeking help from the secretary and the custodian had not been in his official game plan. But it was beginning to look as if he needed them more than vice versa. They might be able to point out barriers and gateways on Pico's political road map. He felt both excited and apprehensive about his new course.

His apprehension dissipated quickly in the first few minutes of his meeting with Phyllis Gleason. She agreed to meet as soon as he asked, though with little apparent enthusiasm. Rodriguez felt awkward at the beginning, but after a few pleasantries he got right to the point. "Phyllis, how long have you been at Pico?"

She responded instantly. "It'll be going on twenty-six years next March."

"So you've had plenty of opportunities to learn how things work here."

"I guess so."

"Could you bring me up to speed?"

Phyllis smiled broadly. "I'm glad you asked. You know, Mr. Bailey asked the same question when he was new. The first thing to understand is that, except for some young teachers, this place has been pretty stable. Most of the old-timers have been together for years. They're friends. They stick together, particularly when threatened by an outsider."

"Like me?" asked Jaime.

"Well, *you* started off with a sermon about high standards and children as if the old-timers had never thought about those things before you rolled in. In their minds, that's exactly what they've been doing for years."

Jaime squirmed as he realized once again the errors of his opening speech. He listened carefully as Phyllis shared her years of experience. Things started to fall into place. Gleason helped by pointing out that Jaime had things in common with some teachers. He and Margaret Juhl graduated from the same teachers college, albeit at a different time. Sam Shepherd and Rodriguez were both Rotarians. Many of the black and Latino teachers had been waiting for a long time for someone to champion concerns about better instruction for students of color.

Later that morning, in the maintenance office, Bill Hill confirmed much of what Phyllis had shared. He added more. Hill had grown up in the neighborhood. He knew most parents and community leaders. His friends were on the school board. He knew most students by name. He was in the cafeteria every morning. He befriended "free breakfast" students and served as a big brother for many of them. Rodriguez could see Hill's love for the school went well beyond his official duties as custodian. At the meeting's end, Hill gave Rodriguez the names of two parents who, he said, would be more than willing to host an informal coffee hour to help Rodriguez get better acquainted.

As Jaime mulled over the morning, he was surprised at how productive it had been. He had not anticipated how important Gleason and Hill were or how much they would appreciate being recognized and valued. Both seemed delighted to feel they had something to teach their new principal. Jaime felt a little less overwhelmed. He sensed that he had made two allies and learned something important: Phyllis and Bill really wanted to help their new principal. He just had to give them the chance. Jaime looked forward to reaching out to others who might not be so receptive. He focused on Margaret Juhl. She could be a big help as an ally or an endless pain as an enemy.

At a scheduled breakfast meeting a few days later, Rodriguez arrived feeling tense. Juhl's abrupt opening did not help.

"So, what's on your mind?" she asked. Her tone seemed brusque.

"Well," he said, grasping for the right words, "someday, I'd like to be like you. Someone who's been at Pico a long time and is highly respected. I thought you might be able to give me some pointers about getting there—teach me a few things."

"Look, I'm close to retirement and breaking in a rookie principal is a lot of work. But I'll give you one clue. Phil Bailey had confidence in his staff. He let us teach. He did not blunder in with sermons insulting our professionalism."

Jaime's first impulse was to snap back or to look for a way to speed up her retirement. But he recalled his counsel from Brenda: *"Very few school leaders know how important it is to learn how to facilitate your opposition. Otherwise, your opponents agree to your face, then stab you when your back is turned."* Jaime figured this might be a good time to take her advice to heart.

"Insulting teachers is the last thing I intended," he said, speaking slowly. "I know how important all of you are. I want us to work together to improve things."

"Why not get to know what we're already doing before telling us how to do it better? Did you think they dropped you into a disaster area waiting for a messiah to ride in and fix things?"

Jaime winced. He tried again. "Of course not. Pico is a great school. I'm lucky to be here. I hear you—people felt I was talking down to them. I don't have all the answers. That's why I wanted to meet with you. I need your help. Not just for my sake, but for the sake of our school and kids. Everyone tells me how much you care. If we agree on that, I know we can work together."

Margaret looked at him for a long time. She finally responded. "You're right, I do care about this school. The question for me is whether your deeds are going to match your words. If they do, I'm willing to give you a chance."

As the discussion continued that the climate was still strained. But Jaime continued to listen and probe Margaret's views of where the school had been and where it needed to go. Eventually, they revisited Jaime's speech at the opening faculty meeting.

"I guess I was so eager that I jumped the gun," Jaime said. "I know Pico has a lot of experienced teachers. I hadn't thought enough about how they might react. I'm sure they believe they're doing a good job. I'm the new kid on the block. They have a lot to teach me. I should have said that. I'll admit, your question midstream during my first time with the faculty floored me. But maybe you were just giving me a dose of my own medicine."

"I wasn't trying to make you look bad," said Margaret. "I was trying to warn that you were headed off a cliff!"

"That's clearer to me now. It's also becoming obvious that I'm better off with people who tell me the truth. It would be worse to have people talk behind my back or stick it to me when I'm not looking. Thanks, Margaret. To be honest, I didn't expect this kind of conversation with the former teachers union rep."

"Well, I'm not wearing that hat right now. I want a cooperative relationship wherever it's possible. I *will* fight as hard as necessary to represent the teachers just as aggressively as I did when I was their official representative. Either way, I'll be straight with you."

Juhl confirmed her promise a few days later when she called to give Rodriguez a gentle warning about Sam Shepherd. She even offered hints for how Rodriguez might approach his assistant principal. Though she never said it explicitly, Rodriguez sensed that she saw Shepherd as a negative force.

"Are you aware," she asked casually, "that he's only two years from retirement?"

A meeting with Sam Shepherd a day later ended when Shepherd walked out of the meeting. Shepherd had not said much, until

Rodriguez asked for his support. Then he snarled that he wanted no part of turning a well-run school over to the inmates.

As the door slammed, Rodriguez realized he had to act. Everyone would be better off if Shepherd moved on. Before his next meeting, Jaime did his homework. He touched base with Phyllis Gleason and Bill Hill to learn as much as he could about Shepherd. At an informal meeting, he listened to parents' complaints about Shepherd's rigid and authoritarian treatment of students. Even more important, he had another long talk with Margaret about Shepherd's personal agenda. A week later, when he walked into their second meeting, Jaime got right to the point.

"I know you don't like me very much."

"You said it, I didn't," Shepherd muttered.

"I also understand that you don't think the school is big enough for both of us," Rodriguez continued. "I agree, and so does the superintendent. We want to offer you some options. I have a memo for you that lays out two of them. Option one is that you move to Hillview as assistant principal. It's closer to your home, and you might find the principal and kids there more to your liking. You might like the other option even more. The district is willing to offer an early retirement package. I hear you've wanted to run a hunting camp for a long time. This might provide the down payment."

Shepherd sat in silence, looking stunned. Finally, he mumbled, "I've got to think about it," grabbed the memo, and walked out—this time without slamming the door.

The next day, his signed retirement agreement was on Rodriguez's desk.

Brenda had been right, Jaime thought. You need to map the political topography before making your moves. A slot on the organizational chart may not tell how much someone knows or how much influence an individual wields. Jaime thought back to something he'd read in graduate school about sources of power, and it suddenly made sense. Some people at Pico, like Phyllis Gleason, had power because of their information and know-how. Others, like Bill Hill, were influential because of their friends and allies. Sam Shepherd was powerful because of his control of rewards and his ability to coerce. Phil Bailey still had lingering personal power based on memories of his genial warmth. Jaime himself had the authority built into the principal's role, but that wasn't really enough to do the job. His know-how as a principal was unproven, and he was just beginning to build his own alliances. He had the potential for substantial power as a result of his influence over agendas and symbols. But his first effort to put them into action in his vision speech had flopped. He now had a clearer sense of what had happened and what he needed to do next.

By going out, talking to people, asking questions, and listening, he was able to discover areas of shared interest that made it much easier to work with most of the people in the school. Building coalitions had turned out to be easier than it had seemed at first. But sometimes, as with Shepherd, decisive steps were necessary. He just had to do it without creating a martyr around whom others would rally.

Jaime looked forward to his next weekly visit with Brenda. For a change, he had a tentative triumph to report. Her congratulations felt much better than the condolences she had given him in their previous consultation. His exhilaration was tempered, though, when Brenda told him to remember that winning a battle was not the same as winning the war. He felt she was probably right but still asked what she meant.

She smiled and said, "Let's wait and see how things go from here. But remember, a school and a kindergarten classroom have a lot in common. Like an ocean, you never turn your back on them."

CHAPTER FIVE

The Tracking Wars: School Politics at Work

Joan was almost at the end of her rope. There could not have been a worse day for Roscoe, once again, to act out. As usual, he drew his sidekick, Armando, into his latest infuriating monkey business. The pair were virtuosos of ruining a teacher's afternoon. Joan had tried everything short of wringing both of their necks, with little success. Nothing she had learned in college or business had prepared her for this. Her classroom had been reasonably orderly most of the time since Margaret's first visit. But now it was careening rapidly toward chaos. And she was at a loss about what to do.

Joan wondered if she would have enough energy to finish planning tomorrow's lessons and still meet Larry for dinner later that evening. She was only three weeks into the term, and school was already spilling over into their relationship. Evenings were becoming another vexing challenge instead of a warm and welcome escape. At her last job, the workday started early but always ended in time for dinner, and she rarely took work home. Just as she was asking herself whether a long run or an afterschool glass of wine would be more therapeutic, she was heartened when Margaret walked into her classroom. It was Joan's first adult hello of the day. Most of her time was spent with kids or grading their work. She rarely left her classroom or had adult visitors.

As if by magic, Margaret swiftly sized up the situation.

"Another rough one?" she asked.

"Worse than that," replied Joan. "Another one of Roscoe's devilish romps—with accompaniment from Armando. They literally destroyed the afternoon. I always believed in the idea of inclusion until Roscoe came along. He's a rocket without a guidance system. When he loses it, he's simply uncontrollable. It's been hell! I didn't know how hard some kids could be."

Margaret smiled. "I get at least one like that every year. Deep down, you love them, but they can drive you nuts. When you get through to them, you feel wonderful. But when you can't, it breaks your heart. In the meantime, you've got to keep ahead of it. If you get behind, you have a year of misery ahead of you."

"Too late. I'm already lagging," responded Joan with a dejected look. "What makes it even harder is that Roscoe is a natural leader. When he goes off the deep end, the other lemmings are right behind. And Armando thinks that he's Sancho Panza, following his master to the end. Their shenanigans are contagious."

"I don't know how many times I've seen a pair like that. Experience helps you put things in perspective, but each year brings a new set of Roscoes. Your training never really prepares you for it."

"Well, it helps just knowing I'm not alone," said Joan with a smile. "Everything has felt so overwhelming and stressful. I'm beginning to wonder if I'll ever make it through the year."

"The headaches never go away completely. The heartaches don't either. But that's part of what teaching is all about. Good teachers learn to put troublesome episodes in perspective. Just between us chickens, some people never do. They either get out or burn out. You remind me a little bit of me. My first year teaching, I got lucky. An amazing lady came into my life. She knew more about teaching than I ever hope to know. She taught me a lot, and I've learned a few things since. Some of it might even help with Roscoe."

"I can't believe it." Joan sighed. "They say your first year is like being tossed into a swimming pool. You sink or swim on your own. Maybe I shouldn't even ask this, but do you also give advice on love lives?"

Joan hesitated until she saw Margaret smile warmly. Then she continued.

"I've been going with a guy named Larry ever since I was in college. Things were going fine until I started teaching. He can't seem to understand why I don't have as much time for him anymore. I'm afraid he's about ready to tell me that either Pico goes or he does. How do I convince him that things will get better? Right now, I'm supposed to meet him for dinner in an hour, and I've still got a million things left to do."

Margaret laughed gently. "Well, I'm not much of an expert on how to deal with Larry, because I'm still single. But let me meet this Larry sometime. Right now, though, let's talk about Roscoe."

A week later, Joan was out sick for a day. That was bad enough, but there was worse to come when she returned. Rodriguez stopped her on the way to her classroom the next morning. His news was bad. Roscoe and Armando had been so unruly that the substitute teacher had left muttering that she would never take that class again. Joan could not help feeling miffed by Jaime's suggestion that she attend an inservice seminar on strategies for dealing with exceptional youngsters. Was Jaime blaming her? Was it her fault if the substitute couldn't control the class? Joan decided it was time to develop her own homegrown strategy.

Following Margaret's advice, Joan began by trying to learn more about Roscoe from someone who knew him well. Joan knew just the person to ask. Heidi Hernandez was one of the brightest and most cooperative students in her class. Heidi was wise beyond her years, though she still tended to perform below the incredible potential that Joan saw in her. Heidi often stayed after school to talk to Joan about her own dream of going to college and becoming a teacher—even though no one else in her family had graduated from high school. Joan knew that Heidi and Roscoe lived in the same neighborhood. Equally important, she felt she could trust Heidi.

As class was ending on a sunny Thursday afternoon, Joan struck up a conversation. "You know Roscoe pretty well, don't you, Heidi?" she asked.

"Sure," said Heidi. "He lives right down the street from me. Sometimes we walk to school together. Sometimes, he's real nice. Other times, he's just plain mean."

"Why do you think that is?"

Heidi hesitated for a moment. "This won't get Roscoe in trouble, will it?"

"No, it won't. I'm Roscoe's teacher as much as I am yours. Maybe you know something that would help me be a better teacher for him."

Heidi screwed up her face and thought for a moment about what Joan had said. Then she appeared to relax and started to talk freely.

"I think about him a lot, Miss Hilliard. His mom doesn't fix dinner for him the way my mom does. His father gets mad a lot, and he's always yelling and pushing Roscoe around. You may not know this, Miss Hilliard, but Roscoe really likes being at school. He thinks you're the best. I think he really wants you to like him, but he doesn't think he's smart enough. When he acts weird in class, at least he knows you'll pay attention to him."

As she thanked Heidi, Joan tried hard not to show the emotion she was feeling. She knew what she wanted to do next. The next day, she worried about how her upcoming one-to-one afterschool talk with Roscoe would turn out. As luck would have it, Roscoe was on reasonably good behavior during class. He seemed surprised when Joan asked him to stay for a while after the final bell had sounded.

"Come on, Miss Hilliard, what'd I do? Armando was causing all the trouble. Make him stay after school."

"You didn't do anything wrong," Joan assured him. "I just want to talk to you."

"About what?" asked Roscoe suspiciously.

"About you."

Roscoe reluctantly agreed to stay. At first, he just stared at his feet while shifting his weight from leg to leg, with a sullen scowl on his face. He seemed afraid that Joan wanted to punish him for something. But as Joan began to ask how Roscoe felt about things, he sat down and looked up at her. He seemed to be looking for clues in Joan's expression. Then he started to talk in a low whisper, and Joan was surprised at what came out. He confirmed many of the things that Heidi had said a day earlier. He did not come right out and say it directly, but he hinted that Joan might be one of the reasons that he enjoyed coming to school.

"You're pretty nice," he said. "My last teacher sent me to the office all the time. She said I was a pain. You don't do that, even when I'm bad."

"You know, I like you, Roscoe. You have a lot of spirit. But let me ask you a question. Do you think you're doing as well as you could in school?"

Roscoe blushed and looked down at his scuffed shoes again. "Don't know," he said. "Maybe not."

"Would you like to do better?"

He looked up, shrugged his shoulders, and said timidly, "Don't know if I can."

"I'm sure you can, and you just said so yourself. Maybe we could make a deal. I help you, and you help me. If we work together, you might be surprised at how well you do."

Roscoe smiled for the first time during their conversation. "Think so? OK, Miss Hilliard, it's a deal." Then his expression changed to a look somewhere between earnest and impish. "But talk to Armando too. He's always getting me in trouble."

Over the next few weeks, the results were mixed. Roscoe was not always true to his word, but he did try—and he did improve. At times, it seemed that he simply could not control himself. At other times, Joan could see him doing his best to resist the temptation to do something disruptive. But even when Roscoe was doing his best, Joan realized that he needed more help if he was going to keep his promise for very long. At lunch one afternoon, she told Margaret what had happened with Roscoe over the last few weeks.

"It's an improvement, but I still feel I need to do something more."

"Didn't Jaime offer to send you to that conference on classroom management? I went a few years ago. Even for someone who's been teaching a long time, it's pretty useful. It gave me some neat ideas that really help, especially with students who have special needs. You might take away some good ideas on ways to structure your classroom to give kids better things to do than act out. Don't forget classrooms are political. In that vein, you did a wonderful job in making Roscoe an ally rather than an opponent."

Margaret's endorsement convinced Joan to tell Rodriguez that she would take his suggestion and attend the conference. She had anticipated that the biggest hurdle would be persuading Larry that it was worth her being away on a Saturday. She dreaded one more harangue about being married to her work. The Fates were kind for once, though—Larry had to be away on business that weekend.

Joan almost flew to school the Monday morning after the conference. The program had been even better than she had expected. She had learned that she was not alone in her struggle to manage students like Roscoe, and she came away with at least a dozen new ideas. She also came away convinced that many of the issues went beyond her classroom and would entail changes in school policies. It would require other teachers to view their classrooms differently and alter their teaching practices. She was bubbling with enthusiasm when she turned in her expense report to Phyllis Gleason. Phyllis accepted the report with her usual cheerful efficiency but added an unexpected bit of cautionary advice.

"Joan," she said, "you look just as eager as some of the other teachers who've come back from conferences with a bag of new tricks. Just don't be disappointed if everyone isn't as excited about your new ideas as you are."

Carlos Cortez shared none of Phyllis's caution when Joan talked to him later that morning. Joan had expected Carlos to be supportive. She was thrilled that he was as excited as she was about revising Pico's tracking system and teaching approaches. In fact, he quickly arranged for an informal afternoon meeting at Andy's Café with several other young teachers. Everyone there agreed that something needed to be done.

"We're labeling too many kids and shunting them off into special classes or classes for slower kids," said Carlos. "That just about guarantees that they'll fall farther and farther behind. Even when they're put in regular classes, their tag follows. And it's particularly the minority kids who get labeled. The district's new inclusion policy is a step in the right direction. It's way overdue, really. But there's too much foot-dragging. We all agree on the need for change but this is a schoolwide issue."

"What bothers me is that they're trying to be inclusive without giving teachers the support they need," Joan replied. "Here I am in my first year. I've got some very challenging kids, and I really need some help. I've been wondering, 'Why me?' Am I wrong, or do older teachers figure out ways to get those students assigned to someone with less seniority?"

"I've sensed that," replied Carlos. "If you believe in inclusion, you wind up with all the students other teachers don't want. We really need everyone to get behind the policy and make it a schoolwide pledge. Otherwise, we're just creating a new form of tracking."

Everyone at the table agreed with Joan and Carlos. When they left Andy's later, they had all made a commitment to weave the district's inclusion policy into Pico's philosophy. Carlos and Joan enthusiastically went to work to develop a presentation to the faculty.

Their optimism grew when they talked to the principal. He applauded their initiative and encouraged them to move forward. When they made their presentation to the faculty, they expected some questions and criticism, but they were stunned by the outpouring of anger and resistance that swept quickly over the gathering.

Phil Leckney led off by questioning whether younger teachers understood what they were getting into. "Look, guys," he said, "I've been to a lot of conferences too. The eggheads in the universities always have some great new idea to save the world, but I've spent a lot of years in the trenches. Those professors aren't talking reality. A lot of them have never taught in a public school classroom. Let them try to do what they tell us to do."

Vivian Chu, always known as a staunch advocate of high academic standards, jumped in to support Leckney. "When we say that all children should learn, we sometimes wind up focusing all our attention on the children who aren't and forget those who are. Besides, those with special needs can disrupt an entire class. The district has already cut funds for gifted and talented. Who's standing up for them? We have to provide a challenging education for our brightest kids. If we don't, their parents will pull them out, and we'll lose those who provide a model for everyone else. Then there's all those kids in the middle. Sometimes they're the forgotten majority."

Leckney's and Chu's views received immediate support from a number of veteran teachers. Even Margaret and Jaime seemed powerless to turn back the tidal wave of staunch resistance. The meeting ended in a stalemate, and a visibly shaken Joan grabbed Margaret on the way out of the room to ask in a trembling whisper if they could talk later. Margaret asked Joan to give her a call in the evening.

On the telephone that night, Joan got right to the point. "Could you believe that today? We're trying to help students who aren't being served. A lot of those teachers are locked in concrete. They put their own convenience ahead of the needs of kids. Just because they can't handle a mixed classroom, they oppose every effort to move forward."

Joan was surprised by Margaret's candid response. "I wish that you had talked to me before the meeting. I could have predicted the response you'd get."

Joan was as surprised as she was disappointed. "Are you saying we should have just kept quiet? Whose side are you on, anyway?"

"I'm on your side, because I think you're right," said Margaret, "but I understand where the others are coming from. This issue is not just about students. It has a lot to do with the same thing you're concerned about—managing the politics of differences. You remember how the battle lines were drawn between you and Roscoe. The standoff began to change when you took time to understand his side of things and make him an ally. You've got a similar situation here. But instead of a difference between two individuals, we now have a potential war between two faculty groups. People are starting to rally the troops to make sure their interests triumph. You have a political problem. You need a political strategy."

"This isn't about politics; it's about students. Why should I need a political strategy?" Joan asked skeptically.

"It may sound cynical, but it's also realistic. We have two groups with different beliefs, and both are struggling for what they think is right. But we'll all lose if the school turns into a battleground—kind of like your early classroom experience."

"So, are we supposed to just back down?" asked Joan with more than a hint of annoyance in her voice.

"No, just get smarter politically. One of the things they never teach you in graduate school is how to understand political tugs and pulls. But you must have run into this kind of thing in your old job."

"Sure, but the office politics was one of the reasons I wanted to get out of there and into a classroom. In a brokerage, people are always looking for an edge, always trying to outdo everyone else. I figured teachers would be different."

"Not as different as you thought," Margaret replied. "When I was in my second year of teaching, the union went out on strike. First time in the district's history. I went out with most of the teachers, but some of the veterans reported for work. I couldn't believe the hatred on the picket lines—the yelling and name-calling. I'll never forget talking to one teacher a couple of days before the strike. She told me that no matter what happened, she was coming to work. She said that the students were more important than a few more dollars in her pay-check. After it was over, a lot of her old friends wouldn't even talk to her—they avoided her in the halls. It took a *long* time for the school to recover. I knew I had to learn more about conflict and why it was so hard for people to deal with."

"So what did you do?" asked Joan with curiosity.

"I asked around, and somebody finally told me about a book that had a couple of chapters on organizational politics. I was skeptical until I read them because I figured, hey, I'm a teacher. This sounds like the stuff principals read when they want to know how to manipulate us. But I devoured that whole book because suddenly a light bulb came on. As teachers, we all work in organizations, and half the time we can't figure out what's going on, because no one ever teaches us anything about how they work. We get a lot of stuff about psychology, teaching methods, lesson plans, and curriculum—the technical stuff that's important in the *classroom*. But they don't teach us about the politics of classrooms and schools."

"But why is all that important if what you care about is what happens in your classroom?"

"Two reasons," said Margaret. "The first is that the classroom is sort of a miniature organization in its own right. I was surprised when I started to think about it that way. Some things fell into place that never made sense before, and I started to see a lot of new possibilities for teaching and classroom management. Think about the struggle between you and Roscoe. People had tried plenty of coercion and punishment before, and he just kept getting more resistant. You started to get somewhere when you negotiated with him. The second reason is that the way the school and the district work as an organization makes a big difference in your classroom. The debate over the inclusion policy is just one example."

"I'm still not with you," replied Joan with a puzzled look. "What's the connection between organizations and the inclusion policy?"

"Look at it this way. Politically, a school is a collection of coalitions—a bunch of different groups, like teachers, administrators, students, and parents. Each group has its own beliefs, its own values, and its own interests. Every group wants certain things, but their interests don't always line up very well. For instance, a lot of parents think what's right for their child is right for the school. As a teacher, you want to do everything you can for their child, but you also have to respond to all the other children in your class."

"But that means parents aren't really a coalition. They're a bunch of individuals," protested Joan.

"Sometimes and sometimes not," said Margaret. "Coalitions come and go, depending on the concern at hand. On some issues, the Pico teaching staff is really together, but right now, the inclusion policy is not a unifying influence. Instead, you've got a couple of coalitions forming within the teaching staff."

"Maybe, but so far I don't see that you're telling me anything I didn't already know."

If Margaret detected the impatience in Joan's voice, it seemed not to bother her. She continued cheerfully. "OK, but here's where I think it starts to get interesting. If you want to understand what's really going on around something like the inclusion debate, you need a different lens to make sense of the situation."

"Meaning what?"

"You want Pico to make a full commitment to the district's inclusion policy. Some people agree, others don't. You start by asking who the key players are: Who is likely to make a difference in how the issue gets resolved?"

"OK, there's the teachers. Some are with us, some are against us, and some haven't made up their minds."

"Right, and that last group might be critical," said Margaret. "Who else?"

"Jaime Rodriguez, he's with us. We know that Dr. Hofsteder, the superintendent, is on our side. Then there are parents, but a lot of them probably haven't thought very much about the issue. Once they hear about it, they'll probably break into different camps, depending on how they think it affects their own children."

"Now we're making progress," said Margaret. "As you're talking about the players, what you're saying is starting to make sense. We can't do anything unless we have enough people behind it. The good news is we have some powerful allies, like the principal and the superintendent. But the opposition is pretty strong too. So, we might win, but at a high price. The war could be pretty gruesome. Once you understand that, you can start to think about other options besides all-out combat."

"Like what?"

"Negotiation, for one."

Deep down, Joan felt very uncomfortable with all the talk of power and combat. She really wanted to believe that a teacher could remain above the sordid world of politics. Yet Margaret made sense.

"I don't know. Negotiation sounds like what you do when you're buying a used car, not when you're trying to help kids."

Later that night, Joan wrestled with Margaret's closing suggestion—befriend your enemies. "You could start by meeting with Phil Leckney," Margaret had suggested. Joan wondered if she and Leckney could even have a civil conversation. Yet Margaret was right. It wouldn't help to tear the school apart. Joan also wondered why Margaret had suggested talking with Phyllis Gleason before the meeting with Phil. But the most persuasive thing that Margaret said was, "If you're going to be consistent with your philosophy of dealing with differences among kids, don't you want to practice what you preach in dealing with your colleagues?"

To Joan's surprise, her meeting with Phyllis was a lot like her earlier meeting with Heidi Hernandez. From Phyllis, Joan learned a lot about Phil and the other teachers who were on his side. Joan got a clearer sense of how they could block the ideas so important to her and her buddies. Phyllis also helped Joan get a better understanding of what "the opposition" was really concerned about. For example, Leckney was not so much against the new proposal as he was fearful of anything that would make it harder to stay on top of an already challenging group of students.

Margaret's offer to facilitate the meeting between Joan and Phil turned out to be a good idea. It was clear that Margaret had been in similar situations before. She opened the meeting by focusing on the issue rather than on personalities or people's feelings. She also set some ground rules. Both groups, she said, were committed to a quality education for Pico's students, but they had different views on how to do it. She suggested that they start by having both Joan and Phil each talk about their views, insisting that they focus on what they wanted for students, instead of what they didn't like about the other's stance.

As they talked, Joan was surprised to find more areas of agreement than she had expected. As the conversation deepened, Leckney acknowledged some of the challenges that he and others were grappling with.

"It's changed an awful lot since I started," said Phil at one point. "When I was young, I felt like I came to teach and the students came to learn. That's not how it is anymore. The neighborhood's more run down. We've got a lot more poverty, a lot more single-parent families, more and more kids who barely speak English. We never used to have to worry about weapons or drugs in the school. Maybe I should have been trained as a social worker or a cop. It's tough enough managing the students I've got."

As Joan acknowledged her own struggles with classroom management, she and Phil felt a bond for the first time. She learned from Phil that part of the opposition to her proposal came from fear that it would just add to the burden of teachers who already felt overwhelmed. Many teachers were genuinely doubtful that the new approach would work. They remembered other "improvements" that had flopped and made things worse. They worried, in fact, that the proposal might overwhelm teachers and lead to an overall reduction in the quality of instruction.

Margaret then raised the possibility of a pilot project as a way to learn more about how the new approaches might work. That would give the teachers who believed in the proposal a chance to experiment and let others have a chance to wait and see whether their fears and concerns were justified.

The meeting ended on a high note. Joan and Phil agreed on the importance of student achievement and classroom management. Even though they disagreed on the potential impact of the district's inclusion policy, Phil supported the idea of the experiment. Joan, Carlos, and a small group that called itself the "True Believers" formed to develop plans for the experiment. On learning of the group's name, some of the veterans playfully chose to label themselves the "Wise People." When one of them teasingly suggested that "True Beginners" would have been a better name for the other group, Carlos retorted immediately, "Does your group spell *wise* w-h-i-t-e?" The zingers hit home, but there was laughter on both sides. Joking and teasing became a playful way to acknowledge the tensions and build bonds between the two different groups.

With enthusiastic backing from Jaime Rodriguez and no serious opposition from their colleagues, the True Believers plunged into the effort with enthusiasm. Unknown to everyone at the time, the inclusion issue was only the tip of the iceberg in a larger problem of student discipline at Pico. While the pilot project moved ahead, new clouds formed on the horizon.

LEADERSHIP LESSONS II

Mapping and Mastering the Political Terrain

Educators often view politics with a mixture of distaste and dread. They hope that their school or classroom will somehow rise above the petty world of conflict and self-interest to the noble heights of reason and virtue. Like it or not, power and conflict won't fade. The question is not whether classrooms and schools will be political but what kind of politics they will have. Those who ignore and avoid power and conflict simply leave the field wide open for the less squeamish. It makes much more sense to understand the political landscape and to develop skills that enable you to be a full-fledged participant in the inevitable give and take. There is productive ground between Mugger's Alley and Pollyannaish naïveté, and effective leaders are able to work in that groove.

Schools are political because they are inevitably a loose collection of different individuals and groups with enduring differences in background, beliefs, and agendas. People differ by role (for example, parents, teachers, administrators, students), by discipline or grade level (counselors, special education teachers, resource teachers), by race and ethnicity, by social class, and by ideology (for example, beliefs about how best to teach reading or mathematics). A second essential feature is scarce resources. There is never enough money, time, or human energy to do everything or give everyone all they want. Choices have to be made. Money spent on athletics can't be used to buy textbooks, and vice versa. Someone has to teach in the grade levels where high-stakes tests are mandated, even if no one really wants to. A principal has only so much time in a day and can't review a budget, calm an angry parent, discipline a wayward student, and lobby the superintendent all at the same time.

The interplay of different interests and scarce resources inevitably leads to conflict. Sometimes competing differences can be resolved amicably through reason and data. More often, they are rooted in deeply engrained preferences, values, or beliefs. It's like asking Catholics and Baptists to agree about papal authority: There's little that the two groups have in common. In such cases, power and political sophistication become critical.

In coaching the new professionals, Brenda Connors and Margaret Juhl posed three central questions:

1. *Who are the key players?* Who are the people, or groups, who care about the issue at hand? Will they care enough to support or oppose you? Who will, or might, make a difference in how things turn out? Whose help is necessary? Whose opposition is too important to ignore? Who on the sidelines can be recruited as an active, supportive ally?

2. *What is the interest of each key player or group?* That is, what stake does each competitor have in this issue? What does each want, and what can you do to help them get at least part of what they care about?

3. *How much power do players have?* Who is likely to have the greatest influence over how the issue plays out? What are the sources of power, other than formal authority, for each key contestant? Who could become a valuable ally if their power was mobilized? Are there any "sleeping dogs" better left undisturbed?

The answers to those questions can be arrayed on a two-dimensional figure in which the vertical axis represents power and the horizontal axis represents position, or interest. This makes the political terrain accessible. The map allows you to make much more informed choices about what to do. In developing an approach, you can consider strategies typically employed by effective politicians:

Look Before You Leap

There are many ways to size up a school before accepting a job. School visits and private off-the-record chats with teachers, students, parents, and administrators can help. Talking to local education reporters can assist in providing background. The Web may provide helpful archival information. Seek out the school's priest or historian for a narrative of past events.

Start Slowly and Scope Out the Lay of the Land

Use your eyes, ears, and other senses to identify powerful individuals and groups. Identify their interests, what they want, and what they will do to get their way. Every organization is political, and you can't lead without suiting up and getting out on the field. There is a zone between naïveté and Muggers' Alley where principals and teachers can be a positive political force.

Clarify Your Agenda

You are more effective when you have both a vision of where you want to go and a strategy for getting there.

Build Relationships and Alliances

Work on building relationships with key players. Spend time and find out how they think, what's important for them, and what they would like from you. The better your relationships, the more likely you are to build support and defuse opposition.

Soothe and Learn From the Opposition

Machiavelli advocated centuries ago: Hold your allies close; hold your enemies even closer. We tend to hang out with those who think like us. That draws a tight boundary between *us* and *them*. A more productive strategy is to open a dialogue with opponents, facilitating their contrary opinions and listening carefully for points to be considered as well as areas of potential agreement. Make sure that you understand how they think and what they care about. Acknowledge the importance of their views. Encourage them to talk to people with whom they disagree.

Embrace Conflict and Deal Openly With Differences

No organization works smoothly all the time. Conflicts arise around even mundane issues. Most principals and teachers shy away from conflict. They avoid it, try to smooth things over, or pretend that it doesn't exist. Usually it just festers and gets worse. People need a chance to voice their concerns and to hear those of other people. Otherwise, differences descend into personal animosity, backstabbing, and street fights.

Negotiate

Politics is a process of give and take. It is a game of trade-offs in which the players compromise in order to reach a mutually accepted agreement people can live with. No one gets everything they want. But pacts allow a school to move forward with most people aboard. When you know what you and other key players want, you're ready to talk about win–win solutions. Optimism and persistence can work wonders when guided by the question: What can we do that works for as many people as possible?

No organization exists without political issues that require a leader's attention. Relying only on authority to get things done never works. As Harry Truman once quipped, "If you can't stand the heat, get out of the kitchen."

Reflective Questions

1. What are the most significant areas of conflict in your school? How are they dealt with? Are they discussed openly? Shoved under the rug? Negotiated in backroom deals? Caught in endless stalemates? Solved through naked power plays?

2. What are the major coalitions or alliances in your school? What do alliances form around? Teaching philosophy? Age and seniority? Race and ethnicity? Are you involved in one or more coalitions, or are you on your own?

3. What is your personal stance toward politics in your school? Do you find them scary? Annoying? Fascinating? Do you want to get in the game, or would you rather avoid the whole thing? Do you try to exercise leadership, or do you wait for someone else to take the initiative?

PART III

The Human Resource Frame

CHAPTER SIX

Sagging Morale

T he controversy over the inclusion policy gradually subsided. The True Believers continued their experiments in creating more inclusive classrooms. The Wise People mostly continued business as usual. But the acute tension between the two groups subsided, replaced by more upbeat discussions about the classroom and teaching. Jaime even saw evidence that some positive changes were afoot. Life at Pico flowed smoothly over the next few months. Even so, Connors warned Jaime to expect more turbulence. As the holiday break approached, he wondered if she had been too pessimistic— until he was blindsided right after the holidays by a powerful new tempest that seemed to come from nowhere.

Jaime always prided himself on his people skills. He found it hard to believe that morale could drop so precipitously. The signs were unmistakable: teachers coming late to faculty meetings, not showing up for parents' night, or resisting playground and cafeteria duty; students acting out and disrupting classes. Roscoe, Joan's miracle turnaround, was spending more time in the office with his sidekick Armando than in class. Both boys had been suspended twice. Jaime was particularly stunned by an anonymous newsletter that viciously attacked him, complete with not-so-subtle ethnic slurs. At the end of January, he knew it was time for another long talk with Brenda. Swallowing his pride at having to admit that he should have paid more heed to her earlier warnings, he called and scheduled a dinner later that week. He and Brenda met at El Ranchito, a popular restaurant not far from her school. Over the appetizer, Jaime briefed her on the latest crisis. She did not seem surprised, but made no mention of her earlier warning. Connors noted that sags in teacher morale following the holidays are not unexpected.

But then she asked a more pointed question: "How's *your* morale?"

Jaime thought carefully before replying. "Not so good. Maybe it's, as you say, just an expected slump after the holidays. But that newsletter was a surprise and really got to me. It's hard to believe any-one would do something like that. It had to be someone on the inside. I'd really like to think that my staff members are mature profession-als, but referring to me as the 'Tortilla Kid' is a pretty low blow."

"Why might someone do something like that, Jaime?"

"Racism, what else?"

"I was the first black principal in three different schools, so I know racism firsthand. Sure, there's prejudice everywhere. But I've learned that if you stop there, it doesn't help very much. It's a label, not a solution. You have to go deeper to find out what's eating at people. Someone has to be pretty frustrated to go that far. The way I see it, people are a lot like plants. Plants have certain needs, like light, water, nutrition, and warmth. When their needs are met, they grow and develop their potential. If not, they shrivel and get weird. People are the same. When their needs aren't satisfied, they either withdraw or go for the jugular."

"If you're saying a principal has to be like a gardener, I agree. That's sort of what I try to do. I spend a lot of my time trying to make sure that teachers get the things they need."

"How do you do that?"

"One of the most important things is continuing a precedent that Phil Bailey initiated: I'm out visiting classrooms as often as I can."

"What do you do when you make those visits?"

"I always look for things that can help teachers do a better job. One thing I learned in graduate school is that my job is to be an instructional leader, not a paper pusher. I always talk with teachers about ways to improve instruction. I give them suggestions and feed-back they need to create the kind of school that we all want."

"One way that people are different from plants is that they can often tell you what they need, if you pay attention. Are you sure what you're giving is what they want from you?" asked Brenda.

Jaime realized immediately that he wasn't sure. "I don't know. Maybe I need to find out."

"Remember that each individual is unique," Brenda replied. "Some of your teachers may appreciate what you're doing, because they want feedback. But others might be looking for a sign that you care or a pat on the back. They might not welcome what you're offering. An anonymous newsletter might be a way to get back at you: 'Tit for tat. If you make my life miserable, I'll return the favor.'"

"But if someone is that upset, why don't they just tell me to my face? I've said any number of times that I'm always available. I've asked them to come to me first when they're upset about something I've done."

"Having your door open does not always mean having an open door. Someone once told me about what he called the mystery-mastery model of interpersonal communication. He said that people have a tendency to protect themselves. One way is to blame someone else when things go wrong. But they rarely tell the person they're blaming, because that's too risky. Maybe it's human nature to protect yourself and other people from the truth. But I've always liked the adage that if life gives you lemons, try to make lemonade."

"I've got the lemons. Now what?"

"Maybe you can turn this newsletter incident into an opportunity. It could be a chance to open up the dialogue between you and the teachers. Right now, you're not getting what you need, and some of them probably aren't either."

"You may be right, but where do I start?"

"When I've run into this kind of situation, I've had good luck with bringing in a neutral third party to help get the conversation going, but that might not work here."

"Why not?"

"Because of where the school is right now. You're still new, and the faculty is still wary. They might not trust an outsider, particularly someone you bring in. It might be better if you and your teachers take this on together. You'll need to make sure that the faculty supports and feels involved in the process."

"So how would you begin?"

"Suppose you start by talking to some of the people you trust. Ask them what they think is going on and how it should be approached. When you think about a school as a family, it's important to remember that you don't always have to come up with the solution yourself. Families often work better when everyone shares the responsibility for solving shared problems."

"That's what I try to do at home. But as a new principal, I feel I have to take charge."

"Jaime, in my first year as a principal, I worried about my authority and losing teachers' respect. So, I tried to prove how strong

I was. It backfired. People could tell that I was covering up. I learned from Buzz Sawyer that sometimes the best thing you can do is let other people know how you're feeling. If your school is a garden, you don't have to be the only gardener. Your needs are as important as anyone else's."

"Maybe I've been trying too hard to be superhuman?"

"Exactly. Happens a lot to new principals. Some teachers dare you to do it, because they know you'll fail. One other point: Sometimes, people want feedback. Other times, they just want support and love. When your wife asks you how she looks in a new dress, she may not want a critique. She may just want some reassurance."

The next day, Jaime met Margaret at the mailboxes just as she was leaving school. He asked her if she had a minute and invited her into his office. After asking a few questions about her request for more science supplies, he got to the point.

"Margaret, it's no secret that we have some unhappy people around here. And you know I'm upset about that newsletter. You've always been honest with me. What do you think is going on?"

"I'm as surprised as you are. Things seemed to deteriorate unusually fast after the holidays. Some of our regular moaners started the ball rolling, but it seems like it quickly became infectious, and now almost everyone is fretting about something. The newsletter must be from someone who's pretty upset but didn't feel they could say it directly. I think the gloom and doom has been building for a while."

"What would you think about setting up some informal meetings with small groups of teachers to try to talk openly about what's going on?"

"I'm not sure. It's been a long time since we've done anything like that. It might get people talking more candidly. But I don't think you should initiate it."

"Who should?"

"It should come from the faculty," Margaret replied. "Let me see what I can do."

"Thanks, Margaret. Is there anything I can do to help?"

"If you get invited to a meeting, just show up and stay cool," was Margaret's reply.

Jaime was surprised when an invitation came from Phil Leckney. He and Leckney were not close, even though Jaime had gone out of his way to help Phil with classroom discipline problems. As Jaime arrived at Leckney's home, he was reassured by his host's warm greeting and hospitality. He had gone to a lot of trouble to arrange the event. The real surprise for Jaime came after dinner. The conversation began awkwardly, as if everyone had something to say but was afraid to say it.

Jaime tried to get the ball rolling. By talking about what he was feeling, he hoped to get other people to open up.

"I really want to thank Phil for setting up this meeting. I think everyone knows I was pretty upset by that anonymous newsletter. But that's only the tip of the iceberg and I'm not looking for someone to blame. I'm really hoping that we can get to the bottom of what's happening and what we can do about it."

After another brief silence, one of the veteran teachers responded, "You want to know what's wrong? I'll tell you. You've been here six months, and all I've gotten from you are kicks in the butt. It's like you come in almost every day trying to figure out what I'm doing wrong. Did it ever occur to you that I'd like to hear if I'm doing anything right?"

Jaime felt every eye in the room on him as the group waited for his response. Then it came to him that he felt the same way. "I know just what you mean, because that's how I feel. I can understand how you're looking for a pat on the back, because so am I. You're wondering if I see you doing anything right, and I'm wondering if the faculty thinks I'm doing anything right."

"So we feel you're tearing us down," said Margaret, "and you feel that we're tearing you down. It's like the saying that if you feel like a molehill, you try not to let anyone else be a mountain."

The tension broke, and there was an air of relief, even excitement, as people realized they were all feeling starved for support and encouragement. Several teachers shared their own stories around the theme of deprivation, and the exchange gradually became more open and animated. Jaime was caught off guard when Leckney suddenly interrupted someone else to blurt out, "I've got something I want to get off my chest. I feel even worse than all these others. You made me look like a wimp by criticizing me in front of my students. That's why I put out that newsletter. To get even."

Jaime felt a rush of feelings: a mixture of anger, admiration, sorrow, and even a surprising impulse to protect Leckney. After counting slowly to five in his mind, Jaime asked, "But, Phil, why hit below-the-belt like that?"

"Because that's what you've done to me for the past six months. You seem to save all the warm fuzzies for your Mexican friends. The rest of us get the cold shoulder or a verbal lashing."

Carlos Cortez jumped in. "What warm fuzzies?" he asked. "You're crazy if you think he does special favors for his so-called Mexican friends. He does the same thing to us. I'm still looking for my first compliment from—what'd you call him?—the Tortilla Kid."

Even Jaime started to laugh at that point, though he was not sure why.

The laughter broke some of the tension, but everyone knew the reference to "Mexican friends" had touched a nerve. Jaime chose his words carefully.

"Phil, I appreciate your honesty. I didn't like the newsletter, and I particularly didn't like the part about the 'Tortilla Kid.' Frankly, I thought the whole thing was a cheap shot. But it took guts for you to tell me you did it. And I hear what people are saying—I've been making your lives miserable, and you've found ways to return the favor. We've been working on different wavelengths. You felt that I was trying to catch you doing something wrong. All I was thinking about is how can we make this school better?"

"I care about that too," replied Leckney. "But constant criticism doesn't help me teach better."

"I know how that feels. I understand that I haven't been telling you about all the good things you're doing. What I'm learning tonight is that we all want a place where we feel accepted and cared for. We have some work to do to create that. Even though some of us are Latino, some are black, and others are Anglo, we're all committed professionals, and we all share the same basic purpose. If we work together and be bone honest with each other, we can do it."

Joan was quiet during much of the meeting. She felt numbed by all the tension. She was relieved, though, to feel a new spirit of cooperation as she left Leckney's home on her way to a nearby coffee shop to meet with Margaret. As she drove, she found herself thinking more about her seesaw relationship with Larry than about the school. Margaret had finally met Larry the week before. He seemed genuinely captivated by her stories about teaching. He even shared his own stories about teachers who had been important to him. Afterward, he had given Joan the supreme compliment.

"Honey, I may be out to make a fortune. But in your new career, you're destined to make a difference."

It felt like a breakthrough at the time, but Larry was soon back to his unsympathetic self. Joan had been stung by his harsh tone a few nights later as they met at the pizza shop.

"First of all, you're late. Second, all you want to talk about is what's going on at that freaking school. I'm getting fed up!"

Joan felt embarrassed, guilty, and angry all at once. But she resisted the temptation to strike back. She tried the same advice that had seemed to help with both Roscoe and Phil.

"Do you feel I'm putting the school ahead of you?" she ventured asking.

"It's pretty obvious, isn't it?"

Joan tried to reassure him, to convince him how important he was to her. He listened and seemed to calm down a bit. For a while, it appeared as if they were finally making some headway. But then the conversation ran into an invisible roadblock neither knew how to get around.

"At least we have an icy truce," Joan thought afterward. But she doubted that the war was over. Then she pulled into the parking lot of Cioppino's restaurant and spotted Margaret's car.

Margaret must have sensed Joan's preoccupation because, as soon as they sat down, she casually asked, "What's on your mind?"

"Larry, more than anything."

"I enjoyed meeting him the other day."

"Oh, he felt the same way. Afterward, he sounded as if he was really beginning to understand why my work is so important to me," Joan said with a sigh.

"You don't sound that pleased."

"I was, but it didn't last. Now he's back to grumping again."

"What about?"

"It's always the same. I don't have time for him. I can't let go of my work. I'm putting everything else ahead of him." She paused. "Maybe he's right."

"It sounds like you both need things that you're not getting from the other."

"I know that," Joan said with annoyance. "We talked about that. It seemed to help for a while. But I don't think we really resolved anything. It's a little like dealing with Roscoe."

"Teaching and developing relationships have a lot in common. What's your biggest concern about Larry?"

"That he doesn't understand me. He doesn't listen. He doesn't really care about my needs."

"And how is that different from what concerns him?"

Silence fell over the booth. Joan saw it right away but hated to admit it. She and Larry felt pretty much the same thing about one another.

"Here's what often happens," Margaret continued. "Something goes wrong in a relationship. We get upset, and we start to blame the other person. Then we start trying to fix whatever we think is wrong with them. We pressure them, try to manipulate them, tell them what they're doing wrong."

"That's pretty much what I'm getting from Larry."

"How well is it working?"

"It just makes things worse."

"Could he feel you're doing the same thing to him?"

"Probably," Joan admitted.

"So there you are. We try to get the other person to change. It doesn't work very well, and then we blame the other person for being defensive and not listening."

Joan was squirming. Margaret's words were hitting all too close to home.

"So," Joan asked, "what's the alternative?"

"Communication. Listening. Working together. Start with the things you have in common. Such as, you want him to care about you, and he wants you to care about him. If you can say that to each other, then you can start talking about what each of you can do to support the other."

"It seems so obvious," said Joan ruefully. "Instead of being honest about what I want from Larry, I've been criticizing him for not giving it to me. And he's doing the same thing. What's crazy is that we're at war because we both feel the same way."

"It happens all the time. It's easy to forget that a relationship is always a two-way street. You need to be open with Larry about what you're feeling, but you also need to make sure you understand where he's coming from. When Larry said he was fed up, you could have told him he wasn't half as fed up as you were. Instead, you asked him if he felt you care more about the school than about him. You had a hunch about what he was feeling, and you checked it out. That's when the conversation shifted, right?"

"Yeah. For a little while, anyway."

"It was a good start," said Margaret. "You have to keep at it. You're not likely to see a miracle cure with Larry, or with Roscoe."

Joan felt herself breathe a sigh of relief. She could feel her shoulders and arms relax. She sipped on hot chocolate and thanked Margaret for listening and caring.

Meanwhile, across town, the telephone was ringing in Brenda Connors's home. An exhausted but elated Jaime was on the other end of the line.

"Thanks," he said. "You gave me the nudge I needed. I learned how big a gap you can have between what you think you're doing and what your teachers think."

"I had to learn that the hard way myself," Connors replied. "We all carry around these pictures of ourselves the way we'd like to be. But we don't always live up to our ideas, and a lot of times we don't know when we're not. The people around see what we do, not what we think. I've had a lot of painful lessons about the discrepancy between what I'm doing and what I think I'm doing. The only way I've found to narrow the gap is to get honest feedback from others."

"That's exactly what happened," said Jaime. "And you're right about one thing. Feedback can sting."

"Sure. That's why people don't always ask for it. But it's a case of pay now or pay later. Procrastinate, and the price goes up. The truth often hurts in the short run, but it seems to bring dividends over the long haul."

"Well, I've felt the pain. I hope I'll soon see the gain as well."

LEADERSHIP LESSONS III

Build Relationships and Empower Yourself

Even highly educated and specialized professionals carry their humanity with them when they come to work. They still need to feel safe, to belong, to feel appreciated, and to feel that they make a difference. School administrators sometimes make Jaime's mistake of trying to be superhuman. They suck up as much responsibility and power as they can in dealing with day-to-day burdens—often with plenty of encouragement from their constituents. Our colleague, Mari Takahashi Parker (1993), compared schools in the United States and in Japan. She found that in the United States, principals tended to feel the weight of just about everything on their shoulders. In Japan, staff and students felt a responsibility to make the principal's job easier. U.S. principals worked much longer days, with much of their time devoted to fighting one fire after another. Japanese principals arrived later and left earlier—they couldn't stay too late in the afternoon, because teachers felt it would be disrespectful to go home before the principal left. There's a lesson here: Americans don't have to cling to the Lone Ranger model of leadership. They and their schools will be better off if they share some of the responsibility. The following guidelines can help principals and teachers respond to some of the perennial relationship challenges in schools.

Empower Yourself and Others

When leaders try to do everything, they leave others frustrated and disempowered. The school bogs down because nothing gets done unless the boss does it or approves it. Connors encouraged Rodriguez to open up communication and share the responsibility for making the school a better place. Staff began to feel that their needs were finally being recognized, and feelings of ownership started to spread. Likewise, Juhl demonstrated how to combine caring, honesty, and effective listening to build open, collaborative dialogues.

Much of Margaret's leadership at Pico School comes from a combination of experience and willingness to take initiative on issues that she could just as easily avoid. She doesn't sit around waiting for someone else to fix problems. Like most teachers, she's got too much to do and too little time, so she can't jump on every problem that comes along. But she doesn't let that become an excuse for inaction. By taking initiative and looking for supporters who share her concerns, she helps to make Pico a better place.

You can help your school by looking for chances to contribute, learn, and have fun. Schools almost always have more things to be done than people to do them. Look for opportunities, and grab the most promising ones.

Reach Out to Build Relationships

Spend time with people—particularly with those who seem distant or who disagree with you. When we're at odds with someone else, we often avoid and stop listening to them. The problem is that when we shut down, they shut down as well. When conflict arose between Rodriguez and the faculty, Connors encouraged him to work at understanding the sources of the discontent by getting closer rather than pulling back. Listen to others. Attend to their feelings, concerns, and aspirations. And tell them the truth. It's familiar advice that almost everyone endorses. But it's easier to practice than preach. The primary barrier is fear. We'd say what we think—if we weren't afraid of the consequences. Much of Margaret's ability to be helpful to both Jaime and Joan came from her willingness to risk telling the truth to her boss as well as to her friends—even when she knew they might not like what she had to say.

Ask for Feedback

Without feedback, both principals and teachers become blind to how they're seen and out of touch with how they're doing. The people around us often withhold their perceptions because they're anxious about how we'll respond. Asking is the easiest way to get honest feedback. This takes persistence and skill in framing the right questions. But keep at it and you'll expand your learning opportunities. If you simply ask a friend or colleague, "What did you think about my lesson/classroom management/speech," the first response you get will often amount to vague reassurance ("Seemed fine to me"). Not much help. Follow up with more specific probes: "What do you think worked best?" "What could I have done to make it better?" "How do you think the students reacted?" Persistence makes your requests clear and credible.

Reflective Questions

1. When have you taken a voluntary initiative to make your school better? What happened? What can you learn from the experience?

2. Are there important topics that people are reluctant to talk about in your school? Are there problems that everyone laments but no one does anything about? If so, do any of them represent a leadership opportunity for you?

3. When was the last time you asked someone for feedback? What might you learn if you ask more often?

PART IV

The Structural Frame

CHAPTER SEVEN

Student Discipline: Who's Really in Charge?

February was turning into Jaime's best month yet. The post-holiday morale crisis and the anonymous newsletter led to a series of informal meetings with faculty. The process was challenging but, in the end, exhilarating. Morale was up. So was trust. People were talking to one another. Rodriguez was on a high. Until the bubble burst.

This time the hot button was student discipline. In the old days, Sam Shepherd had been tireless in his efforts to bring young offenders to justice. He had been police officer, judge, and jury, all rolled into one. When teachers sent offenders to Shepherd, the outcome was never in doubt. He kept the lid tightly clamped on the pressure cooker of miscreants. But after he left, the steam began to overflow. Teachers were complaining about not being backed up. There were more fights on the playground and in the lunchroom. Some parents were getting worried about their children's safety.

Rodriguez knew something had to be done. Even though it was tempting to try to show strong leadership with a quick, authoritative decision, he could see the risks: a failure that he'd be blamed for. This seemed to be a perfect opportunity to try out the district's new shared decision-making initiative. The superintendent, Mildred Hofsteder, was a strong advocate for decentralizing responsibility and involving faculty and parents in formulating key decisions. Every school had been asked to establish a faculty–parent council to serve as an advisory body to the principal. Because discipline was an issue of great interest to both parents and faculty, it seemed like an ideal task for Pico's newly formed council to take on.

Meanwhile, Joan Hilliard was pleasantly surprised to learn that, as a new teacher, she had been elected as the council's first chairperson. Carlos Cortez had persuaded her to become a candidate, and Joan was delighted when Phil Leckney also rose to support her. When she asked Phil about it later, his explanation was simple. "I supported you for two reasons. The first is that your business experience might be useful. The second is that not too many people wanted the job. I might as well tell you that some people may support you because they think you'll be a pushover. But I know you better than that."

At the council's first meeting, Jaime charged the group with looking into the worsening discipline problem. He offered them two alternatives as a way to focus their discussion. One was to hire an administrator to replace Sam Shepherd. The other was to develop a new schoolwide approach that would involve everyone—the principal, the faculty, and even parents and students—in implementing a shared discipline code.

Joan was happy to have the issue on the agenda, but she wondered why Jaime hadn't talked to her before presenting the options. She worried her position as chairperson would be undermined if other council members felt the principal was actually running the show.

In subsequent meetings, her fears were confirmed. The council represented various segments of the Pico community, including teachers, parents, and students. The group was diverse, particularly in ideas about discipline. Despite Joan's best efforts, the council soon bogged down in conflict and trivia. There were debates between liberals and conservatives; teachers and parents; those who wanted a single, schoolwide discipline philosophy; and others who wanted to preserve discretion for individual faculty. Two teachers held out for hiring another disciplinarian like Shepherd. Jaime attended every meeting and often behaved as if he were chairing the council. Joan soon learned that some individuals were meeting privately with him to lobby his support for their particular agenda. Joan sensed that she was rapidly losing her authority to be effective as chair. The question was what could she do about it? She once again called on her trusted mentor.

"It's not just you," Margaret said reassuringly, "the same thing is happening in lots of schools. Everyone's talking about empowering teachers and sharing decision making, but people are also telling principals that they're supposed to be strong instructional leaders. A couple of my old friends are principals—they went over to the dark side," said Margaret with a laugh. "They often feel in a bind. They don't want to step on teachers' toes, but they feel accountable."

"I think I see the problem," said Joan. "I agree—the principal *is* supposed to lead. And a lot of the council members feel the same way. As chair, I want to head the group, but without usurping Jaime's authority."

"So it gets very confusing," said Margaret. "You're supposed to be chairing, but the principal is always there, undermining your say-so. It's like a dance where no one's sure who's leading, who's following, and what rhythm you're supposed to be listening for. Some people are trying to waltz, and others are doing hip-hop. Shared decision making is a good idea, but it's tough to make it work."

"But why is it so hard?"

"It's a classical structural problem. No one's sure who's in charge. Is it you or the principal? People tend to figure that the principal is the real boss in a school, so they look to him for direction and answers. Jaime feels the pressure, and he does what a lot of administrators do: He shoulders the load. No one's at fault. But left alone it won't fix itself. You'll have to do something to clarify the situation."

"Like what?"

"Well, Jaime's learning fast. I think he's starting to get it. Maybe you just need to catch his attention."

"How?"

"Quit. Send him a brief note telling him you're bailing out."

"You're kidding! I want to be chair. I think I have something important to contribute."

"I agree, and so does Jaime. He needs you as the chair at least as much as you need to be in the role. Trust me, as soon as he gets that note, he'll see you."

"Then what?"

"Tell it like it is, and don't pull any punches. Just make sure that Jaime understands you're not blaming him, but you don't want to be part of a two-boss system that confuses everyone."

Joan was doubtful that the gambit would work, but she had enough confidence in Margaret's intuition to give it a try. Besides, she said to herself, I don't have a better idea. Her faith in Margaret was soon reinforced. Within twenty-four hours of getting her note,

Jaime wrote back asking for a meeting as soon as possible. Joan went to Phyllis Gleason to make an appointment.

"Boy, does he want to see you!" said Phyllis with a knowing smile. "You don't need an appointment. Go right in!"

Jaime literally bounced out of his chair as soon as Joan walked in. He offered her the warmest greeting she could remember in a long time. Then he got right to the point.

"Joan, I hope you'll reconsider. If you quit now, I think it will set the council back."

Remembering Margaret's advice, Joan knew she didn't want to give in until she was sure Jaime understood the problem. "Let me tell you why I resigned. For me, it's been a no-win situation. I'm not going to continue unless we fix it."

"But you're doing a great job! Where's the problem?"

"Very simple. I've felt responsible for everything because I'm the elected chairperson, but everyone assumed you were really in charge. Every time I tried to do my job, you did something reminding people that you were really running the show."

Joan had feared Jaime would be surprised or even offended at her candor. Instead, he smiled reassuringly. "I think you're right. After I got your note, I talked to a colleague I trust, Brenda Connors. She said the same thing. So we agree," Jaime replied. "We need to clarify the role of the council as well as that of the chairperson. I've got an idea about how we can do it, but I need your help."

"Well, here we go again. You always have the answers. Aren't you interested in my ideas?"

Jaime seemed briefly taken aback, but then he smiled again and openly acknowledged that she had a point. "Look, Joan, I'm new and you're new. We both have a lot to learn. And right now, you might not rate me as one of the most promising students you've seen."

It was Joan's turn to smile—Jaime's wry humor and willingness to admit error were disarming. "Now we're getting somewhere. But I'm not going to continue as chair unless we clear up the confusion about who's in charge. I have an idea about how we can proceed. At the brokerage house we had a similar problem: Who's in charge—the CEO or the vice president of finance? There was confusion up and down the chain of command about who was accountable for what. When the chaos and conflict began to affect the bottom line, the CEO organized an off-site retreat. An outside consultant introduced a process for clarifying roles, responsibilities, and relationships. It's a process called CAIRO. It sounds like the capital of Egypt, but it's really a straightforward way of trying to bring structural issues of roles and authority to the surface."

"How does it work?"

"CAIRO is an acronym. Each of the letters stands for a different role that someone can have in an action or decision. For example, someone, or some group, is ultimately responsible. They get the *R* in Cairo, because the monkey is on their back. A *C* goes to anyone who needs to be consulted. *A* designates someone who has to approve the decision. If someone needs to be informed about the decision or action, they get an *I*. And they get an *O* if they're not involved in the decision."

"OK, I think I understand what you're talking about. I've seen something similar. You set up a chart, like a matrix, with the different people along one dimension and the different responsibilities along the other."

"Exactly."

"I like it."

"If we do it, I need to manage the process," Joan said firmly.

"That's a deal! Let me know if you want me to help. And tell me the next time you think I'm stepping on your toes."

At the next meeting, Joan led the council through the CAIRO exercise. She explained the CAIRO acronym and distributed a matrix. First, she asked everyone to fill it out individually. Then they shared their individual perceptions. It was an eye-opener for everyone. It turned out that there were at least three different ideas about how the discipline policy was supposed to be developed. Implicitly, Jaime believed that it was his decision in the final analysis. Many teachers felt that the responsibility ultimately ought to be theirs, as most of the implementation would fall into their laps. Many parents felt that the council should make the final decision. The group broke into laughter when a parent commented, "This looks a lot like the way my family works." The council then hammered out a responsibility chart based on CAIRO to assure that everyone knew what they were supposed to do and who was in charge of different jobs that had to be done.

Afterward, Hilliard went to Rodriguez.

"You know, the exercise helped. But I realized something even more basic today. The way the council is set up almost guarantees failure. It's the wrong group to develop something as complicated as a new discipline policy. The council is too big, it's too diverse, and it's got too much to do and too little time to do it. The CAIRO exercise showed we have too many people who think they have the *R*. But if you think about it, only some on the council have a big stake in this policy. I think we should make them a subgroup with responsibility for preparing a draft. They could consult with you, with the teachers, with the community, and with students. Then, if I understand how this site-based management is supposed to work, the council should retain final approval rights."

Jaime closed his eyes and clasped his hands to his lips. It was clear that he was thinking hard about what Joan had said.

"Maybe you hit the nail on the head. Maybe I set this up wrong to begin with. When I talked to Brenda, she told me that a group needs to be clear about four things: what it's supposed to do, what authority it has, who it's accountable to, and what it's accountable for. You're right—a smaller group with a clearer task has a better shot at coming up with a draft of a workable policy. The council already has too much on its plate."

"Exactly. So the council can make its job better by delegating this task. But they have to give the subgroup a clear charge."

"I agree. Is part of the charge to make sure that the major players all feel that they were heard in the process?"

"Sure," said Joan. "Let me develop a plan. I'll check it with you and with some of the council members. If enough people buy in, I'll get someone to bring it to the council."

At the council's next meeting, Joan arranged for a parent to propose a new responsibility matrix for dealing with the discipline problem. The parent said at the outset that the proposal had emerged from conversations among a number of people concerned about making the council work better.

"The idea that we've come up with," she said, "is to create a task force. Their job is to develop a proposal and bring it back to us. They will consult with the entire school community and develop an approach that's fair, consistent, and workable for faculty, parents, and students. Then they'll come back to us. We can approve the policy, modify it, or send it back for more work. Once we approve, the policy goes to Mr. Rodriguez, who says he expects to support our decision."

Several council members glanced at Jaime, wondering whether they could believe what they had heard. Jaime acknowledged the glances and said simply, "The only thing I want to add is that I am fully behind this approach."

The new matrix was approved after short discussion. Council members were unanimously ecstatic about the outcome of their deliberations. Joan proudly displayed their modified matrix and congratulated them on a job well done. Pizza delivered by Antonio, compliments of the principal, rounded out the evening on a high note.

What	Who					
	Students	*Council*	*Teachers*	*Principal*	*District*	*Subgroup*
Collect information	C	R	C	C	I	
Develop draft discipline policy	I	C	C	I	O	R
Collect reactions to draft policy	C	C	C	C	C	R
Develop final policy and plans	C	R	A	A	A	C
Implement policy	I	C	R	R	O	

A task force of three teachers and two parents went to work with enthusiasm. After holding many meetings with different parts of the school community, they came back to the council two months later with a proposal that soon drew broad support. After tweaking some details, the council approved the new policy unanimously, and Jamie supported the decision. The district superintendent and school board signed off, delighted their school council policy seemed to be working. Everyone was optimistic that the whole effort was a giant step forward for the school.

The council did not stop there. One parent had commented pointedly, "Before we get too smug, remember that we've been through things like this before with the PTA. We make decisions, but nothing gets done. Someone called it the 'Pico pile,' the scrap heap of policies and programs that get approved but never really happen."

"You're raising a really important issue," Jaime commented. "Who has the R for implementing the new policy? Otherwise, it might fall through the cracks or into my lap."

"That makes sense," said Joan. "We don't want all this work to wind up in the Pico scrap heap. Should the council work on implementation, or should we delegate that back to the discipline task force?"

Jaime felt pleased as the council decided to work through the implementation issues. He felt that he had helped move the process forward without taking over. He planned to tell Brenda that evening.

During a long lunch break on a Saturday shopping excursion, Joan recounted the details of the discipline policy process to Margaret, who seemed very pleased.

"I hope you feel as proud as I do about what you've accomplished. Maybe it's your business experience. Even though you're a rookie teacher, you're becoming a model of what it means to be a teacher leader."

Joan beamed with pleasure. "Well, I really owe it all to you."

"No, you really owe it to yourself. You brought a lot with you, and you learn fast. I think you're in line for rookie of the year. I just hope our colleagues can learn from your example. We're going to run into other issues just as tough as the discipline policy. If shared leadership is going to work at Pico, more teachers have to believe they can take some initiative."

"One reason to do it is that it might help in classrooms as well," replied Joan. "In working out the confusion in the council, I began to wonder whether I have similar issues in my classroom."

"Which ones?"

"Well, I may be doing to my class what Jaime was doing to the council—taking on all the responsibility. Maybe I was training my students to be passive learners, always waiting for my next instructions. I did all the work, and all they had to do was sit and watch. Where else do you see a supervisor shoveling while the workers look on, resting on their shovels? It might not be easy, but maybe I can show them the difference between the R and the C in CAIRO. I could try to structure tasks where I have a C—they should consult me for ideas and suggestions—but they have the R. They'd be accountable for the decisions they make."

Margaret thought for a moment, and then said, "Interesting. Whether we're talking about empowering teachers or empowering students, the basic issues are the same. Maybe you and I should think about doing a schoolwide inservice on CAIRO and how it relates to relationships between students and teachers. We might try to get parents involved too. What do you think?"

"It may even help some of the parents with family issues at home. Many parents think the R is theirs. They constantly nag their kids to do their homework. What if we tell kids they're responsible— the R is theirs—and let parents know the same thing? If the homework is turned in, the kids get credit. If not, it shows up on their report card. They learn fast and dinner doesn't become an every evening hassle session—until report card time. You know, I learn so much every time we talk, but we haven't had many opportunities to work together. This schoolwide look at classrooms from the CAIRO perspective could give us a chance to combine forces—the rookie and the veteran."

"We're already a great team. The rookie is quickly becoming a pro."

Joan savored that comment throughout a quiet evening at her apartment. Larry was on another weekend business trip. Sometimes Joan was almost relieved when Larry was away midweek, since she usually had so much work to do anyway. But a Saturday night alone was a different matter. She wanted to call him, but once again he had neglected to mention where he was staying. There were too many hotels in Atlanta for her to spend the night trying to track him down.

Oh, well, she thought to herself. Maybe it's better that way. If I tried to explain why I'm feeling so good about my conversation with Margaret, he might just tune me out anyway.

The ringing of the phone interrupted her reverie.

"Sorry I couldn't call earlier, honey," said Larry, "but the meeting ran late. Anyway, I wanted to tell you that I love you. What's happening on the home front?"

CHAPTER EIGHT

Standards and Accountability

The tension in the faculty lounge could be cut with a knife. The superintendent of schools, Mildred Hofsteder, rarely visited Pico. When she did, there was always new trouble brewing, at least in the memories of veteran teachers. This time she was here for a special afternoon faculty meeting. There was none of the usual banter as teachers filed in. Dr. Hofsteder stood at the front, flanked by Jaime Rodriguez and an older man with gray hair, a gray suit, and a generally gray appearance.

"Bureaucrat. Probably from the State Department of Education. Here we go again," Phil Leckney whispered to Joan.

"We must really be in for it," she replied. "More on NCLB?"

"Probably. The beatings will continue until teaching improves."

Jaime opened the meeting with brief introductions of the guests before yielding to the superintendent.

Hofsteder wasted no time in getting to the agenda. "You're all familiar with the No Child Left Behind legislation. I'm sure you are also aware that Pico failed to make adequate progress last year. The standards are going up, and Pico is falling behind. Of course, Mr. Rodriguez is not to blame. He's new this year, and I'm sure he's doing everything he can to turn this around."

The message was lost on no one in the room—blame the teachers, not the principal. Joan glanced at Jaime and felt instant sympathy. He looked more pained and embarrassed than she had ever seen him.

"I never want to see another story in the local papers saying that Pico isn't meeting its educational goals," Hofsteder continued.

"Dr. Samuels from the Department of Education is here to update you on the latest standards and requirements."

Samuels droned earnestly into his presentation. Some in the audience were puzzled by obscure references to "LEA's," "AYP," "Part I, Title A," "HQ teachers," and "nicklebee."

"What's he saying?" Joan asked Phil.

"Dunno. The guy only speaks bureaucratese."

Samuels seemed to warm to his subject when he shifted to the topic of accountability, and his next words snapped the audience back to attention. "The State Department of Education wants to be sure that schools understand the seriousness of our new process for promoting educational excellence. There will be no free rides for underperforming schools, principals, or teachers. All children should be learning, and all schools have to make adequate yearly progress. If Pico can't meet its goals, then we'll move resources to other schools, public or private, that can provide the educational support the students need. Or we'll require that the district restructure the school to measure up to our standards."

By the time Samuels wrapped up, teachers were feeling indicted and threatened. When he asked for questions, he got only silence. Joan looked over to Margaret, half expecting her to leap to the faculty's defense, but even Margaret sat tight-lipped. Jaime looked ill. He squirmed but finally regained his composure and thanked the guests for coming to Pico. Hofsteder and Samuels exited, leaving a sullen group and a very quiet room behind. Only when they were out of earshot did the real meeting convene.

"Good God!" Leckney gasped aloud. "When will this end? Didn't our scores go up last year? Why are they telling us we're failures?"

"Some of our scores did go up," Margaret responded. "But they keep moving the goalpost."

"I'm getting sick of it," Phil replied. "The job keeps getting harder and all they do is ask for more. Create school councils. Demonstrate that we're 'highly qualified.' Implement a new drug program. Meet standards that keep changing. They're reducing our teaching to a bunch of items on a multiple-choice test, and they'll punish us if all of our students don't measure up. We have a lot of kids with limited English. How do we expect them to get great scores on a standardized test? We're working our butts off, and our kids are making progress. I don't mind raising the bar, but if you set it beyond reach, they'll give up. Maybe I'm getting too old for this sort of thing, but come on! I'm a professional. I want all our kids to make it. Treat me like I know what I'm doing."

Jaime was surprised at the intensity of his reaction. "That's pretty strong even for you, Phil. What bothers you so much?"

"When you've been teaching as long as I have, you see a lot of things come and go—alternative this, new that, authentic something else. We get fads from the business world. Glorious ideas from the universities. Pet projects from politicians. I'm supposed to implement about a dozen different standards. How do you ever put anything together if you keep throwing out what you did last year? How is one more fad going to help?"

"I know that the fad of the year is a big problem in education," Jaime responded. "You all keep reminding me that we have a Pico pile filled with new programs that fell by the wayside. I know this won't solve all our problems. But I think you all know the reality. We have a mandate that we can't just ignore—this time, it's got teeth. If we don't comply, we're in trouble."

"But that doesn't mean we have to like it," Phil responded, to nods of assent from many of his colleagues.

"No, but we're better off if we can figure out the most productive way to deal with it. How about if we kick this one around a little before we just dismiss it as worthless? NCLB's intent is good—all of us want to make sure that none of our students get left in the dust. It's the tone and details that bother us."

"Maybe so," Phil responded in a more modulated voice. "But you're going to have to do a lot more to convince me that this isn't one more flash in the pan they're trying to stuff down our throats."

Jaime was feeling the heat. He knew Hofsteder's comments had infuriated the faculty, and Samuels's presentation had been a disaster. But they were gone, and the requirements were still in place, backed by a formidable coalition of federal and state governments, the school board, and the superintendent.

"You're right," he said. "We have a trash heap full of all the stuff that floats in and gets tossed out, but hangs around anyway. Only the labels change on the carousel of top-down innovations. When I started here, I thought I had answers to the school's problems. All I did was convince most of you that I was the problem. We're all tired of these solutions that are mandated from above. But we can't just give up."

Vivian Chu jumped in with support. "Jaime's right. We all know that some of our kids are falling through the cracks. And we don't have very good ways of identifying them. We also know that behind our classroom doors, we do pretty much what we want. Remember what's his name? The one who used to teach in Joan's room? His classroom was like a movie theater. All he did was run the projector and keep the kids entertained. I don't know why he didn't sell popcorn. Maybe we do need a little more accountability."

"It's not a matter of being more accountable or giving up. It's what we have to give up in order to be more accountable." Margaret Juhl rose to her feet and spoke with unusual fervor. "We all know what's at the heart of teaching, and that's never going to be measured on a multiple-choice test. Most of you are like me. You became teachers because you wanted to make a difference. And I believe that I do. You can't always measure it with test scores, but over the years I have gathered a lot of confirming testimony from students and parents. We have to deal with this bandwagon of standards and testing, but we need to make sure that we don't gut the soul of what we do. We're not here just to dispense information. Every student is a promise that is ours to help fulfill. We're here to shape young lives, to give all kids a shot at a successful future. Who we are and our faith in our calling are as important as what we teach."

Nodding heads and affirmative responses showed that, once more, Margaret had hit the nail on the head.

Jaime responded. "I agree, but higher purpose aside, we're still going to be held accountable for short-term results. It's not just my butt on the line. Pico's reputation is also at stake. Those test scores end up in the newspapers. Right or wrong, people judge us on those numbers. It hurts us when we get bad grades. Some parents bug out, which 'nicklebee' makes it easier to do. That puts us in a deeper hole. They could even decide to restructure Pico, which basically means getting rid of us and starting afresh with a new crew. Let me propose that we do two things. First, NCLB says we should use methods that have been proven scientifically. How about if we get one group working on the latest research on teaching for results? Vivian, would you be willing to chair that one?"

Vivian nodded in assent.

"Margaret," said Jaime, "would you be willing to lead another effort to work on building evidence around the intangibles we all value. Joan can take this to the parent council to get their support. What do you think?"

"Can I add to that idea?" asked Carlos. "Some of you attended the inservice on critical friends groups. Margaret and I have been talking about starting one at Pico. The whole idea of a CFG is to work together on teaching and learning. It builds on the idea of professional learning communities that we've been hearing about the last few years. Margaret is perfect to take the lead on that."

Nodding heads told the story. Even Phil Leckney seemed to be willing to go along. But the banter at the bar later that night painted a less optimistic picture. It wasn't going to be easy.

As usual, Phil led the initial charge. "Let's face it. Jaime's caught in the middle. He's trying to save his butt by foisting all this off on us. What we need is a stronger leader, someone who would go to bat for us."

Joan jumped in. "Wait a minute, Phil. You're right; Jaime is getting squeezed like an orange. But we're caught in the same vise. And speaking of stepping up, where were you, Margaret? We were all waiting for you to take on the bureaucrat. Why didn't you speak up while he and the superintendent were here?"

"Over the years, I've learned not to attack when there's nothing to win. Bushwhacking Samuels might have made us all feel good at the moment, but what good would it have done over the long haul?"

"Shouldn't the bureaucrats hear how teachers really feel?" asked Leckney.

"That wasn't his mission. He was just a courier, sent to read us the riot act. You could tell he was uncomfortable. Why shoot the messenger? He did his job. If we took him on, we'd get him annoyed, embarrass the superintendent, and make Jaime squirm harder than he already was."

"So now what do we do?" asked Joan.

"Face reality. Pressures for standards and accountability aren't going away anytime soon. There's too much support for legislation that sounds good, makes politicians look productive, and reassures the public. So we're in a dilemma. We have to not only work with the prevailing policies, but we also have to do what we believe is right for our kids. It's dancing on a tightrope. But good teachers have done it for years. They'll still be doing it long after I'm retired."

"Retirement is sounding pretty good to me right now," Phil volunteered.

"Phil," said Margaret soothingly, "you know your wife says that the day you retire, she's moving out."

"You've got a point, but why should I stay if I'm going to be spending most of my time teaching to the test?"

"Phil, I wouldn't stay either if that were the price," said Margaret. "The tests are one way to keep score. Not the only way. To my mind, not the most important way. I keep my eye on the ball, not the scoreboard. If my kids learn what they need to learn, they'll probably do all right on the tests. But the final test that really matters is whether I help them have productive and happy lives. If they do better on that one than on a bunch of multiple-choice items, I figure I've been a success."

"Dangerous thinking, Margaret," Phil responded.

Margaret smiled. "Old-timers like us are dangerous. We're the kamikazes who can keep the pot stirred and help strike a balance between testing and caring. There are a lot of people in this community who've been touched by what we do. If we play this right, we'll get a lot of support from them and from our kids and parents. That's why Jaime's modified version of the inclusion committees makes sense: the True Believers and the 'Show me the data' crowd—the art-driven accelerator and the scientific brake. It lets us buy some time and get our ducks lined up."

"I hope they're not sitting ducks," Phil sighed.

Everyone laughed. And then Joan pitched in, "Only time will tell."

LEADERSHIP LESSONS IV

Align the Structure With the Work

From birth on, we are embedded in a family structure. This system of roles and rules evolves over time as circumstances change. Mothers expect more help from teenagers than young children. Students returning home from their first semester in college no longer accept parental authority in setting curfews. A harmonious family creates a workable arrangement and makes adjustments as circumstances require. When Sam Shepherd left Pico, he left a structural gap in student discipline responsibilities. The school was faced with the question of how to handle a critical challenge. Should a replacement for Sam be recruited? Or should the responsibilities be distributed through a schoolwide discipline code? The Pico school council, after clarifying its own roles and responsibilities, elected to develop a schoolwide discipline policy. In a classroom, a school, or any other group, people like to know where they're headed, who's in charge, what they're supposed to do, and how their efforts relate to others. Putting eager students or talented teachers into a confusing system wastes their energy and undermines their effectiveness. Structural arrangements demand continual attention, just as human needs do. Teachers sometimes figure that the job of social architect is reserved for administrators. Bosses are supposed to develop policies, provide direction, and make sure everyone's on the same page. Sometimes administrators live up to expectations. Often they don't. If administrators aren't picking up the ball, someone had better, or there will be frustration all around.

Clarify Roles

Without coordination and teamwork, the best individual efforts produce a poor outcome. Maybe you remember a time you made an inspired effort that flopped because someone got in your way or didn't come through. It's frustrating for everyone. If you're in a situation where people are constantly stepping on others' toes or pointing fingers of blame, try an experiment. Choose an issue or task where there is incessant confusion or conflict. Follow Pico's example and apply the CAIRO concepts. Create a matrix listing responsibilities in the far left column. Place individual roles across the top. Now have everyone individually assign a letter to each person for every responsibility. Give an *R* to the person who's responsible—the one with the monkey on his or her back. Now assign letters specifying that person's (or group's) relationships to others. Give an *I* to anyone to be kept informed, a *C* to anyone who needs to be consulted, an *A* to anyone who has approval rights, and an *O* to anyone essentially "out of the loop." CAIRO goes beyond an organization chart to pinpoint exactly what people are expected to do and how they relate to others. Any employee can initiate the activity. Administrative blessing isn't essential, though it certainly helps.

The CAIRO exercise done collectively usually produces several important discoveries. It shows that people often have very different views of how things are supposed to work. It reveals who's overloaded or underused, how many levels of approval someone needs before taking action, and who appears to need to be in control. The exercise often clarifies why people are always at each other's throats and why important tasks fall between the cracks.

Design Groups for Success Rather Than Failure

Groups or teams are a basic feature of schools. Every classroom is a group, and teachers often cluster students for instructional purposes. Teachers and administrators participate in a variety of teams and groups, both large and small. Whether you're the leader or a member, you won't have a very good experience in a group that doesn't know where it's going or what it's required to do. Make sure the group is clear about Brenda Connors's four keys to success:

1. What are we supposed to do? (What's our goal? What's the task we're charged to accomplish?)

2. What authority and resources do we have?

3. To whom are we accountable?

4. For what are we accountable? (What are we supposed to produce? A policy? An implementation plan? A written report? An oral presentation?)

Groups need to know their tasks, how their success will be judged, and who will do the judging. Student groups need to know if they're accountable simply to each other or to the teacher. When principals appoint a faculty committee or task force, they need to be clear about its assignment and what authority it has. Is it supposed to make a decision or simply make recommendations? What resources does the group need? Groups with manageable tasks, sufficient authority, and clear accountability have a higher probability of success.

Set or Clarify Goals

Essentially, we're all goal directed. Teachers or students rally to a cause they know about and care about. No one gets energized by goals they don't know, can't understand, or don't believe in. Structurally, the trick is to set explicit, measurable goals that set up a clear, challenging, reachable target. The chief barrier to establishing goals in education is the multiplicity of goals, some explicit and specific, others vague or hidden. Currently the goal of student achievement reigns supreme. Custody and control along with sorting and selecting students into specialized tracks are close behind. Inspiring and developing future potential is harder to pin down because it is amorphous and elastic. Stories and other symbolic forms help to make progress toward this important goal more tangible.

Shape a Structure That Fits

In schools and classrooms, a lot of structure is already in place—defined roles, curricula, assessment procedures, legal mandates, and much more. Some is helpful. Some gets in the way. How do we decide what arrangement of roles and relationships we need? A workable structure has to fit the task and the people who will do it. Structure is definitely not a matter of one size fitting all. A top-down structure with clear rules and specific procedures works for routine, repetitive tasks like ordering supplies, issuing paychecks, and scheduling classes. But the same system breaks down in handling more complex and open-ended tasks, particularly ones that require skill and discretion. There can be value in standardized curricula and proven teaching techniques only if they are offered as tools that teachers can adapt to their specific circumstances. But efforts to improve schools by imposing "teacher-proof" methods have continually run aground in the face of the unpredictable and unique features of individual teachers, students, and classrooms.

Structure can work for or against us, though we're much more likely to notice when it misfires or gets in our way. There are good rules—and bad ones. Brilliant meetings and disasters. Sometimes people in authority know what they are doing; others haven't a clue. More discretion sometimes pays off big. Other times, it produces mammoth screwups. Schools have good and bad goals. The good ones are displayed as virtues. Shadier ambitions are hidden. A workable balance between public virtues and the "real objectives" provides a reasonable focus that people can honor and accept. Finding the right balance is an ongoing challenge. It doesn't do any good to label all structure as bureaucracy and red tape. We need to make the formal system work for us. That's not the sole province of anyone. It's an ongoing dance. When the dance goes well, it shapes arrangements that generally work. Not all the time, or for everyone. But for most people most of the time. It only happens when teachers and administrators stop blaming and learn to dance the same steps.

Coping With Reform

For more than a century, cyclical bouts of reform have tinkered with the structure of America's public schools, often with little long-range impact. Most initiatives have originated from above—district, state, or federal levels. Very few have been forged by teachers or principals in local schools. The mandated changes have operated, explicitly or not, under a general umbrella of restructuring, because policy makers and politicians typically reach for the tangible structural tools near at hand. They develop rules and incentives intended to overcome resistance to change and to channel schools in what they believe are new and better directions. Meanwhile, teachers and principals lament that top-down reforms are out of touch with the realities they face each day. Billions of dollars have been spent with remarkably little impact. NCLB is only one of many examples, but in recent years, it has been the elephant in the classroom.

Surveys regularly show that Americans give high grades to their local schools but low grades to public schools in general.

International comparisons of educational attainment often show the U.S. lagging behind other developed nations. All this hoopla creates more pressure to improve schools and to provide tangible evidence that students are learning. Because they're visible and accessible, standardized test scores have eclipsed other educational outcomes to become the dominant indicator of a school's performance. In the face of demands for evidence and accountability, schools can't just circle the wagons. Instead, they need to develop an active outreach strategy. Creative school leaders will find a number of options, including the following:

1. *Develop and share tangible evidence of other goals the school has accomplished.* Public displays of student work, media coverage of classrooms making a difference, parent testimony about positive growth in students' abilities, attitudes, or behavior, low dropout rates, and other dimensions of a school's impact can offset the predominance of test scores.

2. *Embrace the intent to ensure that every child learns, and launch efforts to set reasonable standards and include students of all abilities in the instructional mainstream.* Pico is off to a good start by commissioning a group of True Believers to investigate and develop new ways of engaging all students, while recognizing the contributions of the Wise People in maintaining tradition and continuity. The faculty also modified these labels to incorporate both the art and science of teaching, the True Believers and the "Show me the data" crowd. Studies show schools that adapt external mandates to align with their own ongoing efforts are far more successful than schools that simply conform to changes imposed from above.

3. *Keep parents and community informed by developing school–parent councils.* Such groups are a structural addition that can serve as a strong communications link for informing parents and the local community about things like the NCLB legislation. Councils also provide a medium for alerting the community when proposed mandates or changes may run counter to local goals and expectations.

Reflective Questions

1. Are there important activities or decisions at your school that are often hampered because roles aren't clear or are in conflict with each other? Could a CAIRO conversation help?

2. Are there structural features in your school that continually get in the way? Why do they persist? Is the structure too tight or too loose? What would it take to understand the causes of the structural glitch and develop a better way of doing things?

3. How do you balance pressures for accountability and "teaching to the test" against your own sense of professionalism and what your students need? Do you have a workable way of dealing with these tensions? Does your school?

4. How do you and your colleagues cope with mandates from above—particularly the ones that you disagree with? Do you advocate for your perspective? Go along to get along? Ignore as much as possible? Quietly resist? How does your strategy work for you and your students? What other options might you consider?

PART V

The Symbolic Frame

CHAPTER NINE

The End of the Year: Symbols and Culture in Schools

Jaime Rodriguez and Brenda Connors met for dinner at a sidewalk café on a beautiful evening in May. For Jaime, it was a chance to thank Brenda for all her help. For her, it was a chance to congratulate a star pupil on a very successful first year. That done, Jaime turned to a lingering issue—the ghost of Phil Bailey.

"You know, even though I feel good about what we've been able to do this year, I don't understand why there's still so much talk about Phil. It's like his ghost runs the school. One thing I'd like to do before the end of the year is exorcize his haunting presence."

"An exorcism might work," said Brenda with a twinkle in her eye, "but there's another way to think about it. It's human nature to get attached to things and people that are important to us. We even bond to things we don't especially like—like devils or scapegoats. We blame them for problems we don't understand. When an attachment is broken—if you lose a job, get divorced, or move to a new city—you feel the loss. Do you remember times when you lost something you cared about?"

"Sure. When my grandmother, *abuelita,* died. A long time ago, but I still miss her."

"How did you feel at the time?"

"Lots of things," replied Jaime. "Very, very sad. And I remember I got really angry when my dad told me she was gone, as if somehow it was his fault that his mom died. I was in denial because I didn't want to believe it, and at the same time, I was looking for someone to blame. It was real tough."

"Sure. A death in the family might be the biggest loss of all. But you can feel loss even with something that doesn't seem so important. Remember the caboose at the end of the train? It isn't there anymore. There's a little electronic box that's a lot more efficient than the old caboose and its crew," Brenda pointed out.

"Wait a minute," Jaime said. "I used to love waving at the caboose when I was a kid."

"That was a long time ago, but you still miss the caboose. Phil Bailey is Pico's caboose, and you're the electronic box. Most cultures have figured out that transition rituals or ceremonies help people deal with loss. When people die, we have wakes, flowers, funerals, and mourning periods closed off with some form of commemoration. When people get married, we have an elaborate ceremony and a big party to mark the transition."

"Marriage is a loss?" asked Jaime.

"There's something lost and something gained in any major change. People get married for love and companionship, the desire to have children, and lots of other positive things. But marriages get into trouble because people have trouble letting go of old identities and mature relationships. That's why there are so many jokes about in-laws. It can take years to make the transition complete."

"So that's why people are still thinking about Phil Bailey?"

"He was at Pico a long time. It's not surprising that people still miss him. Change is a little like what happens when a trapeze artist has to let go of one bar before grabbing the next. It's scary to let go, but there's more danger in hanging on too long."

"Does that mean maybe we need a funeral for Bailey?"

"Something like that," Brenda replied thoughtfully. "Even though people know you're the principal, it's harder for them to accept it until the torch has been symbolically passed. What did they do to mark Phil's retirement?"

"Nothing, actually. They wanted to hold a retirement dinner, but Phil said he wouldn't come."

"That's too bad. An event is important not just for him, but for everyone else. People need a chance to celebrate both Phil's accomplishments and his screwups, to savor the memories, and to tell stories. They need to say 'Thank you,' 'We care about you,' and 'Good-bye. We wish you well.'"

"But Bailey didn't die," said Jaime. "He retired. He doesn't need a casket. He's having too much fun on the golf course."

"But for many people, his retirement still feels like a death in the family. To them, he's gone. They've never had a chance to mourn his loss or celebrate his life at the school, so it's harder for them to cut loose. If people haven't let go of Phil, it's hard for them to form attachments with you."

"So maybe I need to plan a funeral and see if we can get rid of the ghost for good."

"Remember, you're still a newcomer to the school's culture. You haven't paid your dues yet. You need to check in with the key people in Pico's cultural network. They need to plan and bless something this important."

"Who do you have in mind?"

"Didn't you say that Bill Hill is the eyes and ears of Pico?"

"Yes. He's the unofficial message center. I get the point. I need to talk to him. I also need to talk to Phyllis. She's the school historian."

"She may be even more than that. She might be the unofficial priestess."

"Priestess?" Jaime looked surprised.

"From what I've heard," Brenda explained, "Phyllis takes confessions and gives blessings. She keeps confidences. But she weaves what she hears into her portrait of the school. She celebrates events that succeed. She gives comfort when things go wrong. She's like the priests and priestesses in traditional cultures. They were storytellers, and they presided over rites and ceremonies. She may be a key custodian of Pico's cultural roots."

"You make it sound like I'm more like a tribal chief than a school principal," protested Jaime.

"You've got it, and a wise chief, particularly a new one, knows the tribe's spiritual leaders have to be in charge of important ceremonies. Talk to Phyllis. Ask her who should preside over your end-of-the-year ceremony. She'll know. Otherwise, you might shoot yourself in the foot."

The next morning, as Rodriguez lingered over his second cup of coffee, he felt apprehensive and even a little foolish about his meeting with Phyllis. The more he thought about it, the more he worried that Brenda might be leading him into a morass. If she had not been right on so many times in the past, he might have ignored her advice.

When he and Phyllis Gleason met, he opened by saying that he needed her help again. Then he asked, "Is Phil Bailey still the presiding principal?"

"Mr. Rodriguez, I wondered when you'd ask me that. Mr. Bailey was around for a long time. He wasn't perfect, and he had his quirks, but people were used to him. He was like an old T-shirt. It's comfortable and familiar. It reminds you of memories that get better and better as time passes by."

"Is it true that he nixed the idea of a retirement party?"

"Absolutely. Mr. Bailey was not the kind of person who stood on ceremony. He literally walked out on the last day, gave me the keys, and told me to send home the stuff in his office. He didn't even show up for our end-of-the-year party. I think that wounded a lot of us. People have leftover feelings, and he does too. I've talked to his wife a few times. Retirement is tougher than he expected. He calls friends on the faculty a lot to ask how things are going. They're not sure what to say. It's really past time for Mr. Bailey's official retirement party."

"Maybe for both him and me. I feel I've been in his shadow all year long."

"Do you want me to be frank, Mr. Rodriguez?"

"Of course."

"Well, you've done some things to make it worse."

"Like what?"

"Like the time you came in during Christmas vacation, cleaned out the old storeroom, and redecorated it as a faculty lounge."

"But teachers told me how happy they were to have the new lounge."

"People don't always tell you everything. Teachers did like the idea of the lounge. You did a nice job of decorating it. I know you meant well, but you also threw out mementos that some people really cared about."

"It was like a dump in there, stuff piled everywhere, dust, spider webs. You're telling me people thought that junk was important?"

"How would you feel if someone went up to your grandmother's attic and tossed everything out?"

"I think I'm starting to get it. It just never occurred to me that anyone would miss any of that stuff. I meant it as a gesture of how much I support the teachers."

"It was a good idea. I just wish you had asked me before cleaning out the storeroom. I could have told you what might happen. It wasn't the bits and pieces that were so important; it was what those dusty treasures meant to them. You tossed out some fond memories."

"It's clear that I still have a lot more to learn. I hope you'll keep on lending me a hand and teaching me the ropes."

"Since you're asking, let me mention one other thing. Remember parents' night, when you sent the teachers a memo telling them that everyone would be in the gym, instead of meeting parents in the classrooms?"

Jamie looked perplexed. "Sure. The idea actually came from some parents. They thought it would be a lot more convenient that way. Otherwise, they have to wander all over the school, particularly if they have more than one child at Pico."

"Maybe, but it's always been a tradition here for teachers to meet parents in their classrooms. That way, parents can see the children's work displayed, and the teachers can show off their prized domain. A lot of them work very hard on their classrooms, and they're proud of them. At Pico's open house, convenience probably isn't the most important thing for parents or teachers. Maybe they're more concerned about getting a sense of what it's really like in their child's school surroundings."

"Phyllis, have you ever seen *M*A*S*H?*"

"Sure, why?"

"Our relationship is a lot like the one between Colonel Potter and Radar. You're always way ahead of me," said Rodriguez ruefully.

"I just try to do my job. But you can't learn the ropes alone. Don't worry about Mr. Bailey. I'll take care of it, and I'll let you know what you need to do."

Jaime felt a twinge of annoyance at the idea of taking orders from his secretary. Remembering Connors's counsel, he resisted the urge to remind Gleason who was in charge. Instead, he simply said, "Thanks, Phyllis. Let me know what I should do."

Three weeks later, Jaime arrived at his office to find a flyer on his desk announcing the "Fiesta de Pico," to be held on a Friday evening near the end of the school year. The program highlights were to include "Give My Regards to Bailey," "The New Principal's Report Card," and "What a Guy!" Jaime felt his stomach tighten, particularly when he thought about getting a performance evaluation in public. Would this be a celebration or a lynching? Was the priestess going to preside over a human sacrifice? He hoped that Brenda Connors knew what she was talking about and that Phyllis Gleason would come through.

On a warm and beautiful evening in June, Rodriguez walked into the school's multipurpose room. He was bowled over. He had never seen the room look so festive. He tried to guess where all the flowers, balloons, and streamers had come from, particularly because he hadn't signed any budget requests. His attention was drawn to the large banner hanging from the wall that read simply, "Fiesta de Pico: The Beat Goes On!" He noted with relief that the room looked too festive for a lynching. But he was still nervous, because Phyllis had not yet told him what he was supposed to do.

Just then, someone with a familiar voice said, "Yoo-hoo! Mr. Rodriguez, glad you came early. How do you like the decorations?" Not waiting for Rodriguez's response, Gleason took him aside and briefed him on his role in the event. "When Mr. Bailey arrives, shake his hand, smile, and then go find a seat in the back row. The first part of the party is for him. Whatever happens next, keep smiling, and act as if you're having a good time."

Jaime did not feel very reassured, but he had little time to regroup. A large crowd was already pouring into the room: teachers, staff, parents on the school council, even the superintendent and members of the school board. Just then, he was chagrined to see Sam Shepherd and his wife walk into the room.

In his ear, he heard Phyllis whisper, "Go welcome Mr. Shepherd and ask him about the hunting lodge. He's not doing so well financially. Maybe you could schedule a faculty retreat up there to give him a boost."

He gritted his teeth and tried to follow Gleason's instructions. He was more than pleased at Sam's warm response and was stunned when Mrs. Shepherd took him aside and said, "I can't thank you enough for all you did for Sam and our family."

Before he could regain his emotional equilibrium, Jaime saw Phil Bailey and his wife walk in to enthusiastic greetings from everyone. It was the kind of entrance that movie stars make at the Academy Awards ceremony. Remembering Gleason's advice, Jaime went over to welcome Phil Bailey as warmly as possible before taking his seat in the back row.

What followed caught him off guard. The superintendent, Mildred Hofsteder, walked to the podium. She asked Phil Bailey to come forward. She briefly recounted Bailey's years at Pico and then asked the board chairman to unveil the draped object at the back of the room: It was an oil portrait of Bailey, atop his mammoth oak desk. The room erupted in a standing ovation, and Jaime watched as tears streaked down Phil Bailey's cheeks. What he didn't notice was Phil's wife whispering in his ear, "I hope you have a place to put that." Although Jamie felt jealous, he kept smiling and joined the crowd in the applause.

Bailey's speech was brief and emotional. It felt a little too poignant to Jaime, but he could see that many in the audience were deeply moved. He felt an unexpected sense of relief. He began to ask himself what it would take to push a raise for Phyllis through the district office.

Next at the rostrum was Margaret Juhl. Her job, she announced, was to give the new principal his first annual report card.

Heaven help me! thought Jaime, though he forced himself to keep smiling.

What followed was a delightfully humorous roast. Jaime received an E for effort and an N (Needs to Improve) for citizenship. He tried not to wince at his grade of Needs to Improve for "Opening Sermons to the Faculty," or his citation for "Excessive Zeal in Cleaning Out Old Storerooms." His C (average) for the discipline policy felt low to him. But all that passed when he heard the summary recommendation: "Deserves promotion to second-year principal and a new desk."

Juhl then called Jaime forward. Four people shook his hand: Margaret, Phil Bailey, the superintendent, and the board chairperson. Jaime felt a warm flush of joy, but what followed touched him deeply. The entire faculty came to the front of the room. Some of them were off beat and off tune, but their song said it all: "If you knew Jaime, like we know Jaime, oh, oh, what a guy!"

The "fiesta" was not quite over. Joan Hilliard came to the podium to announce that the Pico School Faculty–Parent Council had a certificate to award its principal. She read it: "To Jaime Rodriguez, Our Principal. In his leadership of Pico School, may he ever be right. But, right or wrong, our principal!" She then unveiled a sleek, modern teak desk. The crowd went wild.

After the certificate and desk, the hug from Phyllis gave Jaime the feeling that maybe he was finally the real principal of Pico.

A few days after Fiesta de Pico, an exuberant Jaime was having lunch with Brenda Connors. He had taken special care to let her know that this one was his treat. As Jamie reviewed the fiesta in loving detail, he could see that Brenda sensed his excitement and pride about the event. She congratulated him on his success, and he tried to express how much he appreciated her help.

"It's getting late, and I have another meeting," said Brenda, "but I really want you to know how much I've valued our talks over this year. And I have a little something for you."

As Brenda reached down to pick up the shopping bag she had brought with her, Jaime pulled out a gift-wrapped package from his briefcase. He placed it on the table in front of her as she brought out her own gift.

"Jaime," she asked with a smile, "what's that?"

"Sort of like an apple for the teacher. Open it."

Brenda unwrapped the package to find a book by Richard Rodriguez, titled *Hunger of Memory.*

"It's a very important book for me," said Jaime. "The author and I are both named Rodriguez, though we're not related. We're both Mexican Americans. He tells the story of what he went through in learning to live in this culture. He helped me find my own story. You've helped me take that story further."

On the inside cover, the inscription read, "To Brenda, an extraordinary mentor, with thanks and love, Jaime."

Brenda beamed and wiped away a tear. "You shouldn't have, but thanks. You don't know how much this means to me. Well, don't just sit there, open yours."

Jaime admired the package, then opened it slowly. He broke into a broad smile, even as his eyes welled with tears. There were two items in the package. One was a copy of John Dewey's *Education and Experience.* The inscription read, "To Jaime: You have learned so much this year! I'm proud of you." The second was a small statue of Pico's mascot, the mountain lion, with a plaque that read, "To Jaime Rodriguez, a good friend and a great school leader, from Brenda Connors."

"You could call it recognition for the rookie," said Brenda, "but it's a lot more than that. It's a symbol of what you mean to me and what I know you'll become."

CHAPTER TEN

"I'm Just a Great Teacher!"

"When they unveiled that portrait of Phil Bailey atop that old aircraft carrier–sized desk, my heart fluttered and my eyes welled up. I don't know what it was exactly, but that may have been one of the best events in all my years at Pico," said Phil Leckney. There were nods around the table at Andy's Café among the group of teachers who had gathered for refreshments and conversation after Fiesta de Pico.

"It was fantastic!" Joan Hilliard agreed. "Before tonight, I'd never even seen Mr. Bailey, but I'd heard so many stories about him. It was almost like he was a ghost roaming the halls."

"He was," replied Margaret emphatically. "That's why we needed the fiesta."

"Was this your idea, Margaret?" asked Carlos Cortez.

"No, I wish it had been. I'm not sure who thought it up, but I know Phyllis masterminded a lot of it, with a good bit of help from Bill Hill."

"When the secretary and custodian put together the best party in years," replied Carlos, "it almost puts us professionals to shame."

"Maybe," said Margaret, "but the principal also helped in his own way. He gave it his blessing and stayed out of the way. That was pretty daring."

"Aren't you being modest, Margaret?" Joan chimed in. "You had a big role, too. I couldn't believe how funny you were in delivering the new principal's report card. I can't remember when I laughed so much. Even Jaime seemed to think it was amusing."

For nearly an hour, people shared their favorite stories about the evening. The mood swung fluidly from laughter to tears and back to laughter again. It was Carlos Cortez who broke the magic spell with a more serious observation. "You know, this is the first occasion we've had this much fun in a very long time. We don't do this often enough."

"Yeah," added Phil Leckney, "and the sad part is that the merriment was for Bailey and Rodriguez, not for us. Why should administrators get all the glory?"

His question struck a nerve and provoked a long silence.

Margaret, looking even more serious than usual, finally said very seriously, "Phil, you just posed the right question. Maybe something's happened to all of us. Teaching used to be magic. It still is, sometimes, but it doesn't always feel that way. Every one of us has probably been at a party and met someone who asks us what we do. We typically get a little embarrassed and say, 'I'm just a teacher.' That's absurd! We ought to be the proudest people on earth. Yet we're taken for granted and we've stopped believing in ourselves."

"Just look what you read in the papers. Schools are failing. Teachers can't teach. Test scores are abysmal," Leckney chimed in. There was bitterness in his voice.

"Maybe it's partly our fault," replied Margaret thoughtfully. "We ought to embrace teaching as a sacred profession. *We* don't take enough time to recognize what makes our job so special."

Joan agreed. "Margaret's absolutely right! This is my first year, and I've already lost some of the spirit I had in September. I love my students. I feel good about how my class went, despite some rough spots. But we don't take time as a group to laugh, cry, share our stories, and have fun together. We did that in my last job. I kind of miss it. If something's not there for *me,* how does it feel after you've been teaching twenty years?"

The strong emotion in Leckney's voice surprised everyone. "You really want to know? You get more burned out every year. A lot of times you struggle just to get up in the morning and make it through the day. You all know I wasn't crazy about our new principal or about some of the ideas he was pushing. I'm not a fossil. I don't resent new blood. God knows, I need a transfusion once in a while. But I need something so that I don't just coast my way to retirement."

"How about you, Margaret?" asked Joan.

"Maybe I pretend a lot. My union responsibilities once kept me busy, and I'm pretty good at mediating battles among different factions in the faculty. But when I close the classroom door, I sometimes wonder if I'm really making a difference. I used to be absolutely sure of that, deep down in my heart. Now, I sometimes question . . . come to think about it, I could use a lift myself."

"Well," said Joan, "if we can have a huge celebration for our principals, why can't we have something like that for teachers? Are principals more important than we are?"

"Of course not!" Carlos responded forcefully. "What matters most at Pico, the moment of truth, is what happens in the classroom between us and our students. Joan, you've got a great idea! I love Jaime, and tonight's fiesta was wonderful. But we should do something for ourselves as well."

Then, to everyone's delight, Phil ordered a bottle of imported champagne. "In the Navy," he said, "there was always champagne whenever we launched a new ship. We're kicking off something just as important. It deserves a toast!"

Andy, the café's owner, returned with a bottle. He sheepishly asked Phil if a California champagne with a French name would qualify as imported. Everyone laughed as Phil expertly scanned the label. He nodded his approval and Andy, obviously relieved, popped the cork.

Throughout the summer, the group continued to meet, gradually transforming themselves into an informal planning team. Initially, they had wondered how Jaime would respond to their plans, but, as it turned out, the strength of his enthusiasm made him one of their strongest backers. His only suggestion was that they add Phyllis to the group. "She knows how to do celebrations," he said confidently.

It was Phyllis who first suggested that some students from Pico's past be included in the fall's opening day ceremony.

"You know," she said, "we've had so many students that we might have written off but who have gone on to do fabulous things. Take Carla Correa, for example. She's the anchorwoman on Channel Five. Or, how about Becky Bernstein? Who'd have thought she'd become a successful neurosurgeon?"

"You must be putting us on," said Phil. "Not Becky! Anyone but Becky! She was the shyest, most off-the-wall nerd who ever graced Pico's hallways. We all thought she'd end up as part of life's invisible woodwork. Becky doing brain surgery? Did she have one herself?"

"Becky not only does brain surgery; she does it very well," responded Phyllis with a hint of indignation. "Try another one. I'll bet none of you know which graduate of Pico is now teaching at Harvard University."

Several tried to guess, but no one hit the mark.

"Charley Packer," said Phyllis finally.

That seemed even harder to believe than the idea of Becky Bernstein doing brain surgery. Everyone seemed so stunned that they could only roll their eyes in disbelief. Phil's almost inaudible whisper broke the silence.

"Well, I'll be. I thought he'd be in the state pen, and instead he cracked the Ivy League. Granted, he was probably the most creative troublemaker I've ever taught. But suppose," he continued in a stronger voice, "those folks don't want to come back to Pico?"

"Nonsense," said Phyllis. "You'd be surprised!"

When September rolled around, the planning group was feeling nervous. They had invested an entire summer designing an opening day event unlike anything in recent memory. Would it work? Would it flop? Would their colleagues think that they were crazy? Only Phyllis seemed to maintain her serene confidence.

Joan heard some of the customary cynical murmurs as Pico's teachers assembled in the front corridor waiting for the opening day's activities to begin. The buzz was not comforting. Few teachers sounded excited to be back, nor did many seem thrilled about what lay ahead. But when the doors to Pico's auditorium were opened and the teachers entered to take their familiar places, the mood changed quickly. There were balloons everywhere, each carrying the name of a Pico student. Crystal apples were on display at the front of the auditorium, each inscribed with the name of a Pico teacher. The auditorium walls were plastered with words and phrases that described the profession of teaching at its best. Huge placards carried terms like *coach, mentor, guide, guru,* and *leader.* There were pictures of previous students everywhere. The room was suddenly abuzz. Even the dyed-in-the-wool naysayers seemed overwhelmed by the banner across center stage. It said simply, "I'm just a great teacher!"

The room was still astir as people took their seats. In prior years, teachers had often settled into a deadening funk in the face of a drone of announcements about new procedures and policies, spiced with a halfhearted pep talk from the principal and an occasional cameo appearance from the superintendent. This time, a different spirit filled the air. But what was it? And what other surprises lay ahead?

As the room quieted down, Rodriguez walked on stage. "Normally," he said, "I would give a back-to-school pep talk, hopefully better than last year's effort."

Murmurs from the crowd confirmed his anticipation.

"But this year, something really different is in store. And now, let the show begin."

Wilma Worthingham, a beloved teacher who had retired a few years earlier from Pico, came on stage followed by a group of almost-familiar faces. As Wilma began to introduce each of the strangers, cries of recognition echoed across the room. "My God! Don't tell me that's Becky," someone said. It turned out that the strange faces had names that were very familiar—at least to the former teachers. Each Pico graduate said a few words thanking the teachers for everything that they had done, but it was Sid Holstrom that brought the crowd to its feet.

"I was probably one of your worst, almost as bad as Charley Packer," he said. "And look at where I am now. Running my own business. Who would have guessed it? I probably spent more time in Mr. Shepherd's office than in class. And look at all the others here who wouldn't be where they are if you had not helped them along when they were here. When you look at us, you see reflections of yourselves. We are your legacy. And we are only the tip of the iceberg. There are thousands more like us who owe you a debt of gratitude."

The ovation that followed seemed to last forever. It was not for anyone in particular; it was for everyone. As the din subsided, Leckney came on. His opening words startled almost everyone present, especially those who knew him as Pico's resident cynic.

"I am a phoenix. I have arisen from the ashes of a burned-out teacher. This year the magic is there again for me. They say that no one can take your spirit; you have to give it away . . . but you can always take it back. If I can reclaim the spirit of teaching, so can anyone here."

Many in the audience were stunned. Someone murmured, "What happened to Phil?" One of Leckney's longtime friends wondered aloud what he had been drinking that morning.

Seeming to anticipate the surprise and skepticism, Leckney continued. "There may be some in the room who wonder if I've gone nuts. I have not. But I'm once again crazy about teaching. I have three years left before I retire. I want to make them the best three years I ever had. I invite all of you to join me."

As Leckney left the stage to sustained applause, a young woman entered the stage came to the podium. Few in the audience knew who she was. With her short, neatly coifed brown hair and tasteful, light blue summer suit, she looked as if she might be on her way to a job interview. She seemed too old to be a Pico student, yet too young to be a teacher. The newcomer walked slowly and hesitantly toward the microphone almost as if she wished that she were somewhere else. But once there, she spoke in a steady voice.

"My name is Rosemary Pulcini. This is my first year teaching, and I'm proud to start my career at Pico. When I interviewed for this job, someone asked me whom I admired most. At that time, I wasn't really sure. But I've had the chance to talk to some of you in the past few weeks and to hear many stories about Pico's students and particularly its faculty. I want to tell you that my heroes and heroines are in this room. I'm looking forward to teaching here for a long time."

The third standing ovation tripled anything ever before seen on opening day at Pico. The meeting then adjourned to the cafeteria, normally a utilitarian spot with an ambiance of aluminum and Formica amid a pervasive aroma of nondescript leftovers. Some teachers wondered if they had made the wrong turn when they found the cafeteria tables decorated with lace tablecloths and crystal candleholders. At every teacher's place were a name card and a large red apple. The event was hosted with gusto by an enthusiastic group of Pico parents. Luncheon was an international buffet featuring dishes from each of the ethnic groups represented at Pico. No detail was overlooked. Carlos Cortez heard one veteran say, "This lunch is better than anything I've ever imagined, even at ten times the cost."

After the lunch, Margaret came to the microphone and said, "I came here twenty-two years ago because of the spirit I felt here. Over the years, that vitality has seen its highs and lows. But I think deep down it's always been here. This year, the Pico glow is back in our hearts, stronger than ever. I would now like to turn the mike over to Pico's principal, Jaime Rodriguez. We are permitting him to say a few words because, frankly, we thought he deserved another chance after last year's opening-day performance."

Laughter filled the room, and Rodriguez was smiling broadly as he came to the lectern. All had been forgiven on both sides.

"What I have to say is very simple," Jaime began. "No school is much better or much worse than its faculty, and that's why I'm so proud of you. We have a great group of teachers here—some like Rosemary Pulcini who are just starting, others like Phil Leckney or Margaret Juhl who have served Pico for a quarter century. It's what you all do in the classroom that produces the results that we were all so proud of. This morning when some of our graduates came back to say thank you, the evidence was overwhelming. Pico has a rich history that we can all celebrate with pride. There have been ups and downs in recent times, and I spent much of last year just getting to know this place and its people. What I've learned convinces me that there are no limits to our future.

"As principal, my job is not to lead the charge, but to support and serve you. Then you can focus your talent and energy on providing the best possible education for our students. Together we can bring new meaning to our watchword, Pico Pride. I want to introduce someone who can say this much better than I because, although new last year, she is now one of you."

Joan Hilliard walked to the microphone. Those who were close could tell she was nervous. Her voice was soft as she began.

"When I came here a year ago, I thought my four years in the business world would serve me well. They did—to a point. But I had a lot to learn about kids and what makes a successful classroom tick. There were times this past year when I wondered whether I could, or should, stick it out. Without a lot of help and support from many of my friends in this room, I would never have made it. But I did, and there's one thing I'm sure of now—I'm just a great teacher, and so are all of you!"

With that said, she placed a small bronze oil lamp on the lectern. With a flourish, she lit the wick.

"Now, it's time to light the lamp of learning to ignite and illuminate our spirit for another year."

From the wings, the student chorus marched confidently on stage. The school song had never sounded better. The cafeteria had never seen so many tears of joy.

LEADERSHIP LESSONS V

Celebrate Values and Culture

Symbols infuse life and work with meaning. In today's modern world, we often lose sight of what Herb Kelleher has called "those important intangibles that mean everything." At Southwest Airlines, history, stories, ritual, and celebration have made the company one of the most successful in the business. Lou Gerstner, former CEO of IBM, agrees: "In business, culture is not part of the game; it is the only game." Culture is even more important in schools. The lag between instruction and outcomes makes teachers' full impact on students visible only years later. Faith kindled by culture, rather than immediate outcomes confirmed by data, defines a good school.

Ceremony is a core aspect of culture. It serves as a theatrical stage for dramatizing values, recognizing heroes and heroines, and telling stories. Ritual and ceremony are convened at important milestones in a school's evolution: high points, low points, and transitions. In the natural course of day-to-day experience, programs and people can be alive and well (flourishing), dying (withering), dead (passed on), or emerging (new starts). Flourishing, fruitful aspects of an organization crave celebration to buoy people's spirits. Fading programs, people, or units call for rituals of support to ease the transition. Comatose people or programs demand rituals of commemoration and letting go. Newcomers or new initiatives need rituals of support and inclusion to weave them into the organization's ongoing cultural tapestry. This evolutionary cycle is a continuous part of all organizations as shown in Figure 10.1. It serves as a template for determining where ritual and ceremony should be convened.

 **Figure 10.1**   Life Cycle

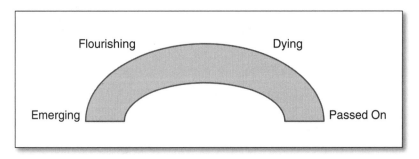

Without ritual and ceremony at appropriate moments, an organization becomes lifeless and sterile or festers with unattended, unresolved issues. Phil Bailey's abrupt departure from Pico left an open wound. His ghost haunted the school, and his replacement remained an outsider until the event that recognized and commemorated Phil's exodus and acknowledged and christened Jaime's arrival as Pico's new leader. Many schools today have grown sterile and toxic because they lack rites to mark important passages. Effective leaders recognize the significance of these events and involve the right people, such as Phyllis, Pico's secretary, and Bill, the head custodian, in making them happen. Beginnings and endings, like triumphs and tragedies, require some form of symbolic recognition. The opening of school, the closing stages of a school year, student achievements, attainment of tenure, a retirement, or the death of a student all cry out for cultural events. The military learned long ago that a change of command has to be marked with pomp and circumstance. Otherwise, the unit suffers, and the new officer struggles to assume authority. When principals come and go without special events, as often happens, schools lapse into cultural emptiness. The seasonal cycles, the highs and lows, and the exits and entrances of school life need special attention and support. So do the everyday accomplishments of teachers and others.

Pico's "fiesta" to let go of one principal and initiate a new one brought home to teachers the importance of celebration. Its success inspired the "I'm Just a Great Teacher" festivity, which became another transforming event in Pico's history. Celebration and ceremony, at their best, are antidotes to boredom, cynicism, and burnout. They bring members of a group together, strengthen bonds, and rekindle a sense of a higher calling and noble purpose. In today's environment, myopic obsession with measurement and short-term outcomes too often overshadows the sometimes magical, long-term influence teachers have on students' lives. The narrow rigor of standardized tests can sap the vigor and vital essence of teaching. Teachers leave the profession or retire wondering whether they have made a difference. Frank McCourt (2005) paints a dismal picture of what too often can happen:

I had an English teacher, Miss Smith, who really inspired me. I'll never forget dear old Miss Smith. She used to say that if she reached one child in her forty years of teaching it would make it all worthwhile. She'd die happy. This inspiring teacher then fades into gray shadows to eke out her days on a penny-pinching pension, dreaming of the one child she might have reached. Dream on teacher. You will not be celebrated. (p. 4)

This same feeling of yearning and self-doubt afflicts many teachers and can infect an entire school. The irony is that while Miss Smith dreams of the student she might have reached, that same student—and others—wish they could thank her for the lingering influence and inspiration carried with them over the years. The "I'm Just a Great Teacher" celebration provided an opportunity to say thank you while teachers were still in the classroom with the chance to reach more students. Together with the other events of the kickoff celebration, this gave teachers a boost to plunge ahead with their good work. Leaders have a moral as well as a practical obligation to support cultural events that perpetuate or revive long-standing values and commitments. They can do this by employing the following tools.

Learning and Celebrating the History

Cultures are created over time as people face challenges, solve problems, and try to make sense out of their experiences. The present is always sculpted by powerful echoes from the past. Frequent glances in a school's rearview mirror are as necessary as having a vision of the future. Every school's history includes a mix of ups and downs, triumphs and tragedies. The triumphs deserve celebration. The tragedies, laced with ample doses of humor, can be turned into stories that are as instructive as they are entertaining.

Diagnosing the Strength of the Existing Culture

Some schools have very cohesive cultures: Beliefs, values, and practices are clear and widely shared, and people are proud of the school and its traditions. In such schools, as soon as you walk through the front door, you're likely to see banners, slogans, photos, trophies, and displays of student work. The message is, "This is what our school stands for. We're proud of who we are, and we want to share it with you." Others have weak cultures: There is little agreement about, or pride in, the school's identity. The only sign you see as you enter may be one instructing visitors to report immediately to the principal's office. Frail cultures often need shoring up; they are an invitation to strong leadership. Robust cultures are the reverse: They resist change and reject newcomers who are seen as enemies of tradition. The good news is that sturdy cultures are usually built on a history of success and progress. That history provides building blocks that leaders can use in crafting the future. But, unfortunately, the educational landscape is littered with too many fragmented or toxic schools that have developed an entrenched culture of blaming, defeatism, and circling the wagons. If you sign on with one of those, you'll need patience, persistence, and a lot of support from somewhere to have much hope of making a positive difference.

Reinforcing and Celebrating the Culture's Strengths

Even in schools with weak or threadbare cultures, it is usually possible to find something worth celebrating. Some alumni have gone on to lead successful lives. There have been star athletes, merit scholars, performing artists, or just individuals whose never-say-die persistence against the odds is worth celebrating. Those stories, values, traditions, heroes, or heroines provide a vital starting point for updating, reinvigorating, and reframing the school's identity and culture.

Telling Stories

It has been said that God's fondness for stories led to the creation of people. Life in organizations generates a stream of rich and memorable narratives. Tales of triumphs and foibles tie past to present, carry values and create images of what the future may hold. As Bateson (1990) concludes, "Story-telling is fundamental to the human search for meaning" (p. 34). Stories cut through the veneer of rational thought and capture the heart. They are truer than true and are as essential to living as food or water.

Schools are chock-full of good stories, some about successes, and others about mistakes or failures. The Beaverton, Oregon, School District relied on storytelling to shape and sharpen cultural values. Annually they convened a storytelling event, inviting tales of the pits and berries of the school year. Both humorous and poignant, the stories elicited laughter and tears. In addition to the joy of the moment, the stories accumulated in a rich cultural tapestry imbuing teachers and administrators with a special sense of purpose and pride in their work.

Incorporating Expressive Language in Everyday Speech and Presentations

Herb Kelleher, legendary founder of Southwest Airlines, peppered his speeches with symbol-laden terminology. To paraphrase one of his speeches, "At Southwest Airlines, you're not just loading bags or taking tickets, you're giving people who could never afford it the freedom to fly. That is our greater purpose, higher calling, or noble commitment." What gave Pico's celebration of teachers such oomph was the repeated reference to the essence of teaching. The profession was lauded with "hot-pink" emblematic language rather than the "pale-gray" terminology of bureaucrats.

Invoking Historically Anchored Symbols

For decades, the symbol of teaching has been the apple. Bringing an apple for the teacher was a practice started in Europe when money was in short supply. At Peabody College of Vanderbilt University, the practice was resurrected in the "Crystal Apple Awards Ceremony." People in the Nashville community and beyond who donated money to the school were given the opportunity to award a crystal apple to a teacher who made a difference. The event soon became a major, citywide event attended by Nashville's mayor and other dignitaries. Pico's happening was filled with similar symbols that gave the event special significance.

Reflective Questions

1. What are the bedrock values of your school community? How are these values communicated? Icons? Heroes and heroines? Stories? Is your school rich or impoverished in its attention to ritual, ceremony, and celebration?

2. What are the most significant cultural events at your school? How well do they work? Could they work better? Are key cultural players involved in planning special events?

3. How often does your school celebrate student or staff achievements and successes? What was the last time your school celebrated teachers and teaching? Was it a special event or merely a routine obligation? Could you do more?

4. Are there unmourned losses or dark clouds that everyone tries to ignore hanging over your school? What kind of ceremony or transition ritual might help your school move on?

5. How do teachers in your school see themselves? How strong is their commitment to the profession?

6. Are teachers absent frequently? Is bitching and moaning a vaunted ritual? Does gossip build up or tear down reputations?

7. How do teachers talk about students? As pains or as promises?

8. What vehicles does your school use to help graduates or parents to recognize the difference teachers are making or have made?

PART VI

Values, Ethics, and Spirit

CHAPTER ELEVEN

Teaching and Leading: Finding a Balance

The spirit of Pico's opening day extravaganza endured well into fall. Teachers said this was the best kickoff they could remember. The school felt alive and energized. People *wanted* to spend time there. Teachers who had never gone beyond their contractual obligation were arriving early to chat with colleagues and prepare for the day. Many parents commented that their children were enjoying school more than ever before. Residents who passed by on their way home from work on fall evenings were often impressed to notice so many lights still on and cars still in the school's parking lot.

The planning team for the opening celebration had grown in numbers with the addition of new volunteers and continued to meet regularly under its new name, the Pico Pride Pack. Everyone agreed that the approaching holiday season was the perfect time for another event—an ecumenical holiday party for the Pico community. Careful planning and a lot of sweat brought their idea to fruition. Phil Leckney, buoyed by his best fall in years, was a jovial and spirited master of ceremonies. Jaime Rodriguez donated what many thought had to be the world's largest piñata. Margaret Juhl brought her still melodious contralto voice to a medley of Hanukkah songs. Heidi Hernandez wowed everyone with her ballet solo from the *Nutcracker*. The students went wild when Roscoe, dressed as Santa Claus and accompanied by his elf, Armando, missed the piñata twelve times in a row. His final effort spread candy and small gifts across the entire cafeteria. Never had the first semester ended on such a high note.

Two weeks later, on a Saturday evening between Christmas and New Year's, Margaret received a tearful middle-of-the-night telephone call from Joan. "Margaret, the bottom just dropped out. Larry and I just had our biggest fight ever. It was the same thing he's been harping on—he's sick of playing second fiddle to my students. He gave me an ultimatum: Either I cut back on my work or he's cutting out. I was furious, but I tried to stay calm. I just said, 'I don't tell you how to do your job. What gives you the right to tell me how to do mine?' He yelled back at me, 'That's it! I've had it!' He stormed out and slammed the door behind him. I am devastated. I thought we were starting to get past all this and that he understood that my work is as important to me as his is to him. He seems to think work matters only if it's all about numbers and bottom lines, but not if it's about children! I don't know, maybe I'll never understand men. Maybe we'd be better off without them. But I've been crying since he left."

The conversation continued for more than an hour. Margaret mostly listened and tried to give Joan as much support as she could. Just before saying good-bye, they agreed to have lunch the next day.

When they met, Joan looked tired; her eyes were red and puffy. She acknowledged that she had sobbed much of the night, but now she seemed more composed. As the two sat together over pasta at La Trattoria, the conversation gradually moved from Joan's breakup to a larger issue.

It was Margaret who signaled the transition. "You know, Joan, as we were talking last night, some real painful stuff came up for me. The early days at Pico felt a lot like they do now. We all did things together, we enjoyed each other, and we did great things for kids. But it also took a big chunk out of our personal lives. You probably wonder why I've stayed single for so long. Partly it's because someone special walked out of my life too, for pretty much the same reasons Larry did. I still wish I'd found a better way to balance teaching and the rest of my life. It's great for everyone to say teachers should take a more active leadership role, but not if it keeps them from enjoying a life outside of school."

Joan was frowning. "Margaret, you sound just like Larry. Why do women have to do all the compromising and balancing, while men just go on doing their thing? If you're a man, you can be committed to your work *and* have a family. Women can do one or the other, but not both. Men get to work as much as they want, and we get stuck on the mommy track!"

"When you put it that way, it doesn't seem fair, does it?"

"It sure doesn't."

"Have you said all this to Larry?"

"I've tried, but whenever we try to talk about it, it pushes too many buttons for both of us. We just get angry and fight. We never seem to get past that to have a real conversation."

"I wish I had the answers," replied Margaret. "It seems to me there's more than one problem here. One involves relationships between men and women. It's about sex roles and about what men and women need from each other. It's also about power and about what it means to be male or female. There's a second issue of overload—we all feel rushed and too busy these days. That can affect any teacher, male or female. Right now, we're stuck—we don't know how to move on either issue."

"Maybe that's just how things are." Joan looked and sounded discouraged.

"Do you really believe that?" asked Margaret.

The question seemed to mobilize Joan's more optimistic side. "No, not really. I'm just down after last night. In fact, an idea just came to me. What if we talk about this stuff at the next Pico Pride meeting?"

"That's a terrific idea. Because maybe what we're talking about here is not problems, but dilemmas."

"What's the difference?"

"Problems have solutions. Dilemmas don't exactly *have* solutions, because you're caught between different values—like between commitment to teaching and responsibility to family. It's not a tension that ever really goes away. You just have to look for better ways to manage it and find a workable balance. That's why it makes sense to talk about this with our colleagues. Right now we're all dealing with symptoms. We need to get a better handle on what's going on and what we can do about it. I don't know of any better way to do that than to talk with some of those who have the same concerns."

At the next Pico Pride meeting, Margaret and Joan presented the issues they had discussed. The nodding heads confirmed that others shared their concerns. On the surface, everything was going extremely well at the school, but something more troubling was brewing underneath.

Phil Leckney led off the discussion. "I'll tell you one thing. You don't have to be female to worry about all this. I'm feeling caught in the middle of a riptide myself. On one hand, I've never felt better about my teaching. My classroom is running better than it has in years. The kids are learning, and I look forward to coming to school every day. But on the other hand, I miss the spare time that I used to have. When I came to school at seven-thirty and left at two-thirty I had time to do other things. I could work on my boat, spend time in the yard, and make a few bucks as a referee. I haven't been near my boat all year. The yard's a mess so it's a good thing it's covered with snow. My wife nags me about needing the extra money."

"Wait a minute, Phil. I understand what you're saying," responded Rosemary Pulcini, "but I'm not sure you really got Joan's message—because you've got a wife. You have someone who takes care of the home front while you focus on your career. Joan and I don't. I know what she's saying. For me, being a first-year teacher is simply *overwhelming!* There's never enough time to do it all. Lesson plans, correcting student work, talking to parents, going to meetings—it never ends. And I'm not sure how long it's going to take before my husband tells me he's fed up. Your wife doesn't work, does she, Phil?"

"Not now, but she used to before the kids." Phil paused and smiled as if to say that Rosemary's message hit home. Then he looked directly at Joan. "Maybe I'll always be a fossil in your eyes, Joan. You're right, my marriage is pretty traditional. But I wouldn't give up on Larry yet. Thinking back, I remember a time when I thought you were always on the attack, and I felt my best defense was to dive for cover. But all that changed when we started to listen to one another. If this old dinosaur can learn from you, I'll bet he can too."

Joan rose from her chair, walked over to Phil, planted a kiss on his forehead, and calmly returned to her seat. Phil turned beet red. Everyone in the room was silent for a few moments before a wave of laughter spread over the group.

"You know," said Phyllis Gleason, "this conversation is a blessing. I've been worried for the last couple of months. I hear things. In one way or another, you all share what Margaret and Joan are talking about. What's happening now is a lot like what happened in Pico's heyday. That was more than twenty years ago. It almost broke my heart. We had drinking, affairs, divorces. This is a déjà vu that I never want to go through again. It's not just you teachers. I was talking to Jaime's wife last week. She was telling me she's worried because she never sees him anymore."

"That's a good point," said Carlos. "We're not the only ones who worry. As we get deeper into this stuff, it's important to include Jaime as well as other teachers and staff. What do you think? Should we invite Jaime to our next meeting?"

The group quickly accepted Carlos's suggestion. At the next meeting, Rodriguez agreed that the issues deserved attention but seemed as perplexed as everyone else. "It's a dilemma. I've never been more proud of our school and what we're doing for our students. But the whole thing could crash if everyone burns out."

"If we all have the same concerns," said Carlos, "why not plan a retreat to see if we can get to the bottom of it?"

"I think it's a great idea," Jaime exclaimed. "I'll talk to the super-intendent about getting some funds."

Joan responded angrily. "Now, wait a minute. Here we go again! If we do it over a weekend, it's another big chunk out of our personal lives."

"You're right, Joan," said Margaret. "It's a real catch-twenty-two. But I think we're going to have to spend some time in order to get more. Another possibility would be to ask the district to cover a day's worth of substitutes. That way, we could spend an evening on Thursday, a whole day on Friday, and a half-day on Saturday. Is that a compromise that people would buy? I think the union could go along with that, as long as it's voluntary for teachers."

"Well, Jaime, it's up to you. You have to sell it to Dr. Hofsteder. Would she buy it?" asked Joan.

"I think so, if the faculty is really behind it."

As it turned out, getting faculty support was relatively easy. Many shared the same concerns and worried about how long the school could continue at the same pace. The superintendent threw her full weight behind the idea. She and the school board were so pleased with what was happening at Pico that they did not want to see their lighthouse project run out of steam.

An expanded Pico Pride Pack planned the retreat and developed a theme—"Thriving and Surviving." As they wrestled with how to organize the event, Margaret offered an idea. "A few years back," she said, "I took a course on school leadership."

"You wanted to be a principal, Margaret?" Phil inquired skeptically.

"No. I just wanted learn more about how they think. And I remem-ber this one framework that's really been very helpful for me. It talks about four main issues that every organization, schools included, needs to address. The first is to create a structure that works. The second is to respond to people's needs and provide the skills that they have to have. The third is to manage conflict effectively, and the last is to develop a shared sense of meaning and commitment. I think each of these may be important to unmask the issues of balance and burnout that we're try-ing to get at. What if we had groups working on each of them?"

"Margaret," said Joan, "this all sounds *awfully* familiar. Haven't I heard this before somewhere?"

Margaret smiled. "You sure have. Many times. They're ideas that worked for me. I hoped they would for us, too."

"Well, I think they've been seeping into my head, even if I didn't always realize it," replied Joan.

"I don't know whether this conversation is a commercial or not, but it sounds like it's worth a try," Carlos commented.

Using Margaret's suggestion, the planning group broke the faculty and staff into groups, each charged with exploring one of four issues: (1) How can we use our time more efficiently? (2) How can we deal with conflict more productively? (3) What inservice training would help or is needed? (4) How can we balance schoolwide cohesion and commitment with family and other obligations?

Despite some tense moments, the retreat was a huge success. A range of issues and feelings surfaced, but they were almost always framed in a way that allowed the group to get below what people were thinking and feeling to the real reasons and move forward. The group produced a number of new initiatives. It also identified areas where more information was needed. The efficiency team identified several structural avenues to make better use of time.

One was to use team teaching to reduce duplication of effort. Another involved reducing the number of meetings that teachers attended. The overall impact was to free up time for individual teachers to do preparation and grading at school rather than taking it home.

The conflict group and the inservice groups collaborated to develop workshops on both alternative strategies for managing conflict and on techniques for time management. The cultural cohesion group concluded that the school needed to sponsor schoolwide events that included spouses, partners, and families to reduce the separation between work and personal life. The group also remembered what the original Pico Pride Pack had demonstrated about the importance of symbolic beginnings and endings. They ensured that the retreat concluded on a high note with a series of skits that left everyone rolling in the aisles. Sam Shepard, whose hunting lodge was the site for the retreat, made a cameo appearance to congratulate the group on its accomplishments: "I wish we had done something like this when I was part of Pico." Coming from Sam, it was an unexpected but welcomed compliment.

People left the retreat feeling optimistic about finding a better balance between life and work. Everyone believed that the school could be a more harmonious place to work and people could make home a more comfortable and supportive haven from demanding jobs.

CHAPTER TWELVE

A Talk About Values

His Wednesday breakfast meeting with Brenda Connors was the most sacred item on Jaime Rodriguez's calendar. As their relationship deepened, both had come to cherish their two-person support group. It served as vital nourishment for both mind and spirit. Over time, they delved ever more deeply into issues that principals often recognize but rarely voice. On a particular Wednesday in February, only a few weeks after the successful weekend retreat, Rodriguez wanted to talk more about values. He had grown up in a family that put a strong emphasis on bedrock principles. His parents always seemed to have clear answers to every complex question of right and wrong. Now that he was a school principal, things often seemed fuzzier. The clear distinction between doing the right thing and compromising personal ideals often seemed elusive.

"Somewhere I heard that the difference between management and leadership is that managers do things right and leaders do the right thing," he mused. "That sounds good, but the choices aren't black and white. How do you *know* what the right thing is?"

"Doesn't it come down to what you believe in and what your values are?" asked Brenda.

"Sure, but that's what I'm trying to sort out," replied Jaime. "It's easy to say that I'm committed to education for all children. I really believe that. But what do I do about Ted?"

"Who's Ted?"

"He's a veteran teacher. Nice guy. Means well. Wants to do a good job. But he's floundering in the classroom."

"What's the problem?"

"They say he used to be pretty good, but he's had chronic health problems. His wife left him for someone else a couple of years ago. Now he's a single parent with three kids. Seems to be in personal meltdown. Chaos in his class, and not much learning. Parents are complaining, but when I talk to him, he says he's getting it together. He's sure he can do better, and he claims he loves teaching."

"Ouch! How long has this been going on?"

"A few years. Maybe one reason teachers liked Phil Bailey so much was that he gave everyone good evaluations. If you look at the paper trail, Ted was doing fine, until I came along last year and rated him 'needs to improve.'"

"I've been there. It's no fun."

"I've been thinking about some of the toughest situations I was up against last year. What made them so hard was trying to sort out conflicting values."

Brenda smiled. "You figured that out more quickly than I did as a young principal. Value conflicts are the mind-numbing tussles. They make it hard to tell the difference between a ball and a strike. It's like shifting from being an umpire who calls them as he sees them to being a philosopher trying to figure out what she believes in."

"Somewhere I read an article that talked about four important values in education," said Jaime. "Excellence, caring, justice, and faith. All of them make sense, but they don't always point in the same direction."

"That's the case with Ted?"

"I'm still trying to sort it out. The first value, excellence, is one that we hear about most. Our job is to help kids achieve as much as possible as measured on standardized tests. My role as a leader is like an engineer or an architect—diagnosing how things are working and figuring out how to do them better."

"No one champions mediocrity," Brenda replied. "But I worry when producing short-term results is the only thing people focus on. A school is not a factory producing widgets. We're dealing with people's futures."

"You put your finger on my dilemma in dealing with Ted. Schools are like families. People have an obligation to care about one another and to look out for each other's welfare. At its deepest, it's the value of love," said Jaime.

"I think we both like to think of principals as servant leaders," Brenda added. "Our job is to understand people's needs and concerns, and to serve them by building a caring community."

"But with Ted I'm bumping into a conflict between caring and excellence. His students deserve a good teacher, and that's not what they're getting. I owe it to students and parents to try to get Ted out of the classroom. But, on the other hand, my heart goes out to Ted. I don't want to put a single dad out on the street with no way to support his family. I don't like what he's doing with kids, but I still want to treat him with respect. If I hurt him, it would set a bad example for everyone else—a callous principal riding roughshod over a struggling colleague. Ted becomes a victim, and I the villain."

"So you're caught between caring and excellence, and you're looking for some way to strike a balance. Is that where the value of justice comes in?"

"Good question. It adds additional weight to the dilemma. The basic idea of justice is fairness. It's like the statue of the blindfolded goddess with the scales. People have a right to fair and equal treatment. I need to be fair to both Ted and his students."

"And fair to parents and other teachers?"

"And even to other principals. One way principals fix this kind of problem is to engineer a transfer of a mediocre teacher like Ted to some other unsuspecting principal. The dance of the dregs, as it's called sometimes."

"Don't try to shove him off on me," laughed Brenda.

"You're too smart to take him, but some others might. But is it fair to dump my problem on someone else's school? Am I my brother's keeper? Or should I just watch over and protect my own school?"

"How much of a premium do you place on justice?"

"As much as on excellence and caring. But it gets even more knotty when I take parents into account. Another aspect of the Ted issue is that parents mostly worry about justice for their own child. The word is out on Ted, so parents try to finesse the system to get their kids moved to someone else's class."

"That makes it even harder for you to champion fairness?"

"It sure does. These value issues are really intertwined," said Jaime. "Everything is layered on top of something else, and a lot of times different layers are pitted against each other."

"But there's an even deeper layer to an already perplexing dilemma—the value of significance," said Brenda. "From that vantage point, the whole process of dealing with Ted becomes a ceremony in search of a cultural beacon for your school community. You want an outcome that restores people's faith in Pico—and in you as principal."

"Looking back, the biggest challenge of my first year was build-ing spirit and restoring faith. That's what I was trying to do with my vision speech last fall. Above all, teachers need to believe they make a difference. We both know a lot of teachers who burned out somewhere along the line. Education is a tough business, and the rewards are so elusive. It's a challenge to keep the spirit and main-tain the faith, particularly when so many people are bashing schools and teachers. Of course, in Ted's case, parents are upset for a reason."

"So all you have to do is provide excellence for students, caring for Ted, justice for all, and, while you're at it, build faith in Pico's mission."

"You got it—it's a tall order," mused Jaime, "But I'm getting clearer as we talk. This is an opportunity, because everyone will be watching to see what happens with Ted. If I can find an approach that's compatible with the first three values, I think the last one will take care of itself."

"Can you pull it off?"

"Not without help. I think part of the answer could be putting some-one like Margaret in Ted's classroom on a regular basis. She might be willing, because it wouldn't take her long to get Ted's class shaped up."

"She might help Ted get back on top of his game?"

"She could. And, of course, I'd have to keep working with Ted on an improvement plan."

"What about Margaret's class?"

"Margaret's at the point where she could get away at times. She could leave a few notes on the blackboard and her class would pretty much run itself, with some help from her student teacher. There's something magical about that woman. Her students would rather miss recess than disappoint her."

"Sounds as if you might have a plan."

"Not unless other people buy in, and I have all the pieces worked out," Jaime acknowledged. "But with some help, I think we can turn this around. It would be a big symbolic victory. Talk about building faith."

"Jaime, that's the most important thing a principal does. Radiate the faith, so others don't lose heart."

"Sounds right, but I sure had some moments of doubt this past year."

"We all do. Every year. But the longer I've been a principal, the more I'm convinced that our primary job is to be a spiritual leader. We have to inspire people to recapture the true meaning of their work, and to revive the things that touch their hearts and souls. Remember the Fiesta de Pico? When the Pico faculty anointed you as their new principal, I got goose bumps. When you're dealing with a generation of children in a school, each day should give everyone an acute case of goose bumps."

Leadership Lessons VI

Problems and Dilemmas

Physicians differentiate three types of patient problems. Type I issues arise when both symptoms and treatment are clear. Type II cases emerge when the problem is well defined, but the solution is hazy or muddled. Type III puzzles are the most troublesome: The symptoms are hard to read, and the remedy is elusive or creates a paradox. Many of the challenges educators wrestle with are Type III problems—hazy issues or dilemmas that pose a potential clash of values.

The bind was highlighted in a 2008 *Newsweek* article, "The Case for Killing Granny." On one side of the debate is the value of perpetuating life; on the other is the imperative to control the spiraling costs of health care. Some experts estimate that at least 30% to 40% of Medicare expenditures occur in the last two years of individuals' lives (and others peg the percentage even higher). This quandary creates intense advocacy from proponents on both sides of the conflict. The absence of any real negotiation or compromise has paralyzed efforts to reform America's health care funding and practices.

Dilemmas trap leaders between a rock and a hard place, with potentially negative consequences of any choice they make. In 2009, Howard Schultz, the CEO of Starbuck's, confronted a thorny dilemma in the face of a recession and softening in his chain's business. Should he introduce more financial controls and standardization in hopes of improving efficiencies? Or would he do better to focus on restoring the entrepreneurial, creative culture that made the company unique. In the August 6, 2009, edition of *Business Week,* an article titled "Starbucks: Howard Schultz vs. Howard Schultz" highlighted the intensity of the conundrum:

> When he reclaimed the responsibilities of chief executive in 2008, he announced that Starbucks had lost its way: it had become the kind of soulless corporation he detested. He promised to take the company back to its roots, to make Starbucks loved again. He has had to acknowledge, however grudgingly, that the company needed to change almost everything about how it operates. (p. 30)

Striking a balance between culture and costs, soul and standards, is never easy because competing values are at odds. Individuals face either/or choices, and risk being impaled on one horn or another of value dilemmas. Leaders need the capacity to operate comfortably in the middle of such struggles, always searching for a fulcrum point on a precarious teeter-totter or new way to frame the issue that provides an escape route from the dilemma.

Education Is a Complex Business

Educators continually grapple with problems without solutions and solutions without problems. Teaching and learning are complex, and many of the toughest challenges—such as balancing caring and achievement or teaching as a science versus teaching as an art—are elusive. There are plenty of solutions bandied about, each with its own constituency in or outside of schools. But the proposed remedies often show little understanding of the problem being addressed. To amend an ancient Roman adage: "While the public and policy makers fiddle, educators flail." Most of the knotty issues in schools involve tough choices between competing values. Leaders need to recognize dilemmas in order to know what they're up against. It is tempting to treat Type III problems as if they were Type I, with a clear diagnosis and solution. That is a path to failure and disappointment. Physicians facing similar challenges are constrained by the Hippocratic Oath: "Above all, do no harm." Don't implement a cure (solution) that is worse than the disease (problem). Talented leaders, like wise physicians, must be accomplished diagnosticians, able to differentiate between problems, solutions, and dilemmas. Problems are solved typically through rational analysis; dilemmas are best handled politically and symbolically. Sizing up a situation adequately is the first step in developing wisdom and helps prevent costly errors. It helps when leaders are able to don several hats: counselor, social architect, politician, and poet.

Every classroom is a miniature community, and each school is a distinctive culture. Trying to balance excellence, caring, justice, and faith is an ongoing dance on a wobbly tightrope. But the moral obligation to attend to these intangible issues is the centerpiece of leadership. In schools, the costs of falling short are too enormous to measure. At risk are the lives of children and the future of our society. To succeed in this awesome responsibility, leaders have to step outside their comfort zone and grapple with what's right and how to make the right things happen. There is no recipe for how to proceed. As we say in the title, this book is a guide for the path to school leadership. If you follow the well-traveled road you might arrive at a destination. If you cut a path, you may leave a trail.

Reflective Questions

1. Which, if any, of the values of excellence, caring, justice, and faith is honored in your school? What other values are significant? How clear is your school on what it stands for?

2. Which values are most important to you personally? How do your own values align with those of your school?

3. How well can you discriminate between problems and dilemmas? Do you know the difference between doing things right and doing the right things?

4. Does your school have chronic dilemmas or value conflicts that never get resolved? What are the values at stake? Do you see possibilities for making headway in dealing with the competing values and options?

PART VII

The Torch Is Passed

CHAPTER THIRTEEN

The Essence of Teaching: Leaving a Legacy

No one expected it. Margaret was close to retirement, but everyone assumed that she would go on forever. The news that she had cancer knocked the wind out of everyone in the Pico community. Each day, people waited for an update on her condition. Had the surgery been successful? Was the chemotherapy working? When would she be back to work? What if she never returned?

Phyllis Gleason became a human hotline for news about Margaret's progress. Bill Hill served as the primary link to parents and the community. Grapevines sometimes distort the news in the direction of worst-case scenarios, but Pico's gossip network was remarkably accurate and reassuring. Everyone hoped that positive thinking would help Margaret's recovery and speed her return to the school she loved so much.

On a warm and sunny spring morning in late April, Joan Hilliard, Carlos Cortez, and Phil Leckney were among the first to visit Margaret at St. Joseph's Hospital. Phyllis had declined an invitation to come along.

"The best medicine for someone who loves teaching as much as Margaret is a visit from a few of her closest buddies. I know Mr. Rodriguez feels the same way. He and I will be over at St. Joseph's another time. Just be sure to call me as soon as you finish your visit."

As the three teachers walked down the shiny floor of a hallway that felt sterile and smelled of antiseptic, they wondered how Margaret would look and what her condition would be. As they entered Room 203, they were pleasantly surprised. Margaret was propped up in bed with a book, her wire-rimmed, half-circle reading glasses sitting crooked on her nose. The color in her face looked normal, although they suspected that makeup played a role. But the twinkle in her eye and the smile on her face emitted the genuine good-old-Margaret presence that they would recognize anywhere.

"Joan! Carlos! Phil! So good of you to come. I told the doctors if they didn't let me have some visitors, I was going to walk out of here against medical advice. Come on in! Sit down! Tell me the latest scoop. How's my class? Who's subbing for me? Are the kids behaving? Has Jaime been called in on a rescue mission yet?"

Margaret's visitors wondered if they had wandered into an interrogation chamber rather than a friend's hospital room. As the hail of questions continued, they looked in vain for somewhere to sit amid the overflow of flowers, plants, balloons, and gifts. They were hard pressed even to find a place for the philodendron that they had brought as a gift from the faculty. Carlos started to move a huge bouquet of multicolored spring flowers from the chair by Margaret's bed in the hopes of clearing a place to sit.

"No, Carlos, don't move that one. That's from my kids. Every one of them signed the card—can you believe it? Where did they ever get the money to pay for something that gorgeous? Come on, two of you can sit on the foot of the bed. Phil, lean against the sink. I want to be able to see you while you bring me up to date. So what's new at Pico? I'm dying to know."

Everyone winced at Margaret's choice of expression, but Carlos started the briefing, only to be interrupted by Joan with a story about Phil's failed attempt to play a classic "trick-the-rookie" prank on Rosemary Pulcini. Rosemary had caught on so quickly that the hoax backfired and Phil himself became the butt of the joke. Phil blushed while everyone else in the room laughed uproariously. Margaret laughed so hard that tears rolled down her cheeks, streaking her rose-colored makeup. For the next half hour, her visitors talked nonstop, sometimes with all three talking at once.

Margaret took it all in as if she were reconnecting to a vital source of energy from which she had been shut off for too long. As Phil was filling Margaret in on some of the latest community gossip via Bill Hill, Joan saw a hint of pain cross Margaret's face. She gently nudged her colleagues.

"We could go on for hours and that might be just what Margaret wants, but I know the doctors will have our heads if we overstay our welcome."

Margaret seemed both disappointed and relieved when her guests agreed that it really was time for them to go.

"Wait a minute. Before you go, I want you to take these envelopes with you. One is for my substitute, to give her some details of where to find things and some sage warnings about the students most notorious for driving off subs. The other envelope is for my students. I want Horace to read the first part to the class and then give it to Sally for the finale. Horace will be great in getting the funny stuff across, but he'd flub the last part. There's also a note for Phyllis and for Bill, so that they can help get the word around. And this one is for Jaime. He sent me a note a couple of weeks ago asking about some personnel decisions. Tell him I'm sorry I wasn't able to get back to him sooner. I know these things have been bothering him."

As Joan was wondering to herself whether there was any message that Margaret wanted to send to her colleagues, Margaret picked up the book that she had put down as they came in. "The last thing I want you to do is go by Barry's bookstore and pick up some copies of this book, *Teacher Man,* by Frank McCourt. I know a few people have already read it, but all of us should. It's a challenging, bone-honest book. If you stay with it, it really cuts through the day-to-day undercurrent and gets to the heart of what it means to be a teacher. I find that every chapter really gets me thinking about myself and my teaching and reminds me how much I really yearn to get back to my classroom. It would make me feel good to know that others are reading it too. In fact, I'm assigning all of you to read it before the next time you visit."

Her visitors smiled at Margaret's irrepressible compulsion to teach, but promised to do their homework. Each gave Margaret a hug and left carrying the envelopes that Margaret had entrusted to them.

"She looks great," observed Phil as they walked down the hall.

"She does," Joan replied hesitantly, "but even though she seemed like her old self when we got there, she wore out fast. Did you notice the pain apparent in her face just before we left? I'm not sure she's as good as she looks. I just hope she's going to make it."

"Don't even say that, Joan," replied Carlos. "She will. She's got to."

"Why do you think she wants us to read that book?" asked Phil. "I'm not much of a reader myself."

"I guess we'll find out when we read it. You too, Phil. It may do you some good," Joan replied. "Let's stop by Barry's on the way home. It's only about four blocks from where I live. We can get the books before you drop me off. That way we can take them to school tomorrow."

When Margaret's three visitors arrived at Pico the next morning, they were in such demand that they felt almost like visiting rock stars in the presence of admiring fans. But these fans were not looking for autographs. They wanted to know how things were going with Margaret. Joan distributed the envelopes as Margaret had requested. Phyllis and Bill greeted theirs with such enthusiasm that Joan knew they could not wait to begin making their rounds to spread the news.

Two weeks later, Joan was sitting in her apartment on a rainy May evening when the phone rang. When she answered, it was Margaret at the other end.

"Margaret, how are you? You know, you're still the only thing we talk about at Pico anymore. Everyone keeps asking why we were all supposed to read the book."

"That's part of why I'm calling. Joan, I'd really like to talk to you. I know how busy you are these days, but could you find time for another hospital visit in the next few days?"

"Is tomorrow afternoon too soon? Four o'clock?"

"That would be perfect. Just you, OK?" said Margaret.

Joan went to bed still pondering the meaning of Margaret's phone call. Nothing was said directly, but they had known each other so long that they often needed no words to grasp what the other was thinking. Joan hated even to think it, yet she was almost sure that Margaret's call was not a portent of good news.

When Joan arrived at Margaret's hospital room the next day, she was again greeted by the same cheerful Margaret, this time perched in the chair next to her hospital bed. Cards and writing materials were spread in a series of neat piles across her bed.

"Joan, thanks for coming. I'm still writing thank-you notes. It's just amazing all the cards I've received. I was just reading one from a girl I taught more than 20 years ago, and I hadn't heard from her since. Let me clear some of this stuff away so you have someplace to sit."

"How about if I just move the things on this chair over to the window ledge?"

At Margaret's nod, Joan sat down.

"You're looking better every time I see you." Joan tried to sound as cheerful and convincing as she could.

"Well, the truth is I look a little more tired every time you see me. At least that's how I feel. Look, we've never tried to kid each other. The news from my doctor isn't as good as I'd hoped. I probably won't make it back to school this spring. This might have been my last year teaching." Margaret's voice was soft, and there were tears trailing down her cheeks, though hardly visible through Joan's own tears.

Fighting the impulse to break down and sob, Joan came over and hugged Margaret awkwardly.

"Please go sit down!" said Margaret. "There are some things I need to say."

Joan returned to her seat, fumbled through her purse for tissues, and struggled to compose herself.

"I've had a lot of time to think about my life while I've been here, and even more about my career and how teaching has touched every corner of my life. I've been asking myself whether I would do anything differently if I had it all to do over. You tried another career before becoming a teacher. I never even considered other options. And there are a few times when I did something pretty silly or said something that hurt someone else. On these things, I wish I had a second chance. But the thing I feel surer about than anything else is that I made the right choice when I decided to be a teacher. I've started to think about what I'm giving back to a profession that's done so much for me."

Joan knew she should not interrupt, but the import of Margaret's talk about her legacy was too upsetting. Did it mean that she was giving up?

Joan blurted out, "Let's talk about the future, not the past."

Margaret smiled and responded calmly. "The future is exactly what I'm talking about. That's why I wanted to speak to you alone. You're very special to me, Joan. Have you read the book I assigned?"

"Every word. It was wonderful."

"I knew you'd like it. As I was reading the final pages it, it got me thinking again beyond the routine to reflect on the spiritual side of what we do. In earlier times, schooling was basically religious instruction. Somewhere along the line, we lost our way and started to think of schools as factories instead of temples. As teachers, we have a moral obligation to hold on to the essence of what we're about. Otherwise, we stand to lose everything. Frank McCourt has a beautiful way of talking about it. Wait a second—I have the book here. OK, here it is:

> The classroom is a place of high drama. You'll never know what you've done to, or for, the hundreds coming and going. You see them leaving the classroom: dreamy, flat, sneering, admiring, smiling, puzzled. After a few years you develop antennae. You can tell when you've reached them or alienated them. It's chemistry. It's psychology. It's animal instinct. You are with kids and, as long as you want to be a teacher, there's no escape. Don't expect help from the people who've escaped the classroom, the higher-ups. They're busy going to lunch and thinking higher thoughts. It's you and the kids. So, there's the bell. See you later. Find out what you love and do it. (McCourt, 2005, p. 255)

"I love it!" said Joan. "Isn't that what we were trying to get at with our celebration of teaching last year?"

"Yes, that was a great beginning, probably one of the best things we ever did at Pico. But there's a deeper level of what we're about that we didn't quite get to. It's a level we're almost embarrassed to talk about—the spiritual dimension that makes teaching a calling, a job with a higher purpose. It's about values: the values we live by and the values we pass on to our students."

"Isn't caring the core value in teaching?" asked Joan.

"It's critical, but there are other important values that we often overlook. Take Roscoe, for example. You certainly cared about him, but it took more than caring. Being loved was not all that Roscoe needed. He also needed to master some basic skills and learn to set higher standards for himself."

"That makes a lot of sense. One of the toughest challenges I had with Roscoe was deciding when to tell him how much I liked him and when to really push him to do better work."

"In deciding when to support or push Roscoe, you also had to consider fairness for everyone in the class. Roscoe's like a lot of children these days. When they look around them, they feel the world is unjust. You agree. But when you try to make things fairer for one child, you run the risk of creating injustice for others— particularly the kids in the middle. You know how much your students insist on fairness. They want a just classroom."

"That's what happened to me when we finally got Roscoe straightened out," replied Joan thoughtfully. "Some of the other parents complained that their children were getting shortchanged."

"When you try to take all these competing ideals into account, there's always going to be tension. A classroom has to be caring, it has to be just, and it has to value performance and results. But even deeper than that, it has to be a place of hope. It has to have meaning and to build faith."

"What do you mean by faith?" asked Joan.

"Faith is believing in things when everything tells you not to. It's believing in Roscoe even when his record tells you you're fooling yourself. It's convincing Roscoe to have confidence in himself even though almost no one else ever has. It's getting his parents to have faith in him and what school can mean. Even more important, teachers have to believe in themselves and in their work. That's where I think we've fallen down. Just pick up any magazine or newspaper. Listen to the conversations in restaurants. Think about how we teachers talk when we're together. The public has lost faith in us, and we've lost faith in ourselves."

"But what about the opening-day celebration or the holiday party? Weren't we on the right track?" asked Joan.

"Of course. They were both very important. So was the retreat, because it gave us a chance to talk about balancing conflicting values. For me, that's one of the things that makes McCourt's book so poignant. He said some things I'll never forget, and I want to make sure that people remember them at Pico even if I'm not there. That's why I wanted you to distribute the books. And I want you to promise me that you'll have the same conversation with your colleagues that we're having now. It'll be even more powerful coming from you, because you've tasted life on the other side. You chose to be a teacher after trying a career in business. I don't know why I feel so strongly about this, but I do. I have my own religious faith, and it's really a comfort now. But I'm also drawing heavily on my faith in teaching. I want to make sure others carry on these values while they have more time than I do to do good things for kids. Do you promise?"

CHAPTER FOURTEEN

Passing the Torch

J oan's promise reverberated on the drive from the hospital to her apartment. When she arrived to an empty apartment, she had an impulse to call Larry, just to have someone to talk to. But she resisted, remembering how rarely Larry had understood her dedication to teaching. Instead, she picked up Tracy Kidder's *Among Schoolchildren* from a nearby shelf and started to read the final chapter again. As she drifted off, the last few sentences kept replaying in her mind.

> She belonged among schoolchildren. They made her confront sorrow and injustice. They made her feel useful. Again this year, some had needed more help than she could provide. There were many problems that she hadn't solved. But it wasn't for the lack of trying. She hadn't given up. She had run out of time. (Kidder, 1989, p. 342)

It was still dark when the sound of her telephone woke Joan the next morning. Startled, she looked at her clock to see that it was only 5 a.m. She was almost afraid to answer. Her worst fears were confirmed when Jaime Rodriguez said, "Joan, she's gone."

"Margaret? Oh, God, no! What happened?"

"They aren't sure yet. The operation and the chemotherapy took a lot out of her, but even the doctors were surprised."

"I can't believe it," Joan exclaimed. "I saw her yesterday. She looked tired, but I never expected this."

"I'm planning to have a brief schoolwide assembly this morning. I think we should tell everyone at once. I'd like to say a few words and then have a couple of teachers talk about her. I'm hoping to get someone like Phil Leckney or Vivian Chu—someone at Pico who's known Margaret for a long time. Bill Hill will be great because so many of the kids know and trust him. I also wanted you to say something, because I know how close you and Margaret have become."

"I don't know, Jaime. I'm not sure I can do it. I might just stand up there and cry."

"I'm not sure I can do it either, but I figure as the principal, I have to give it my best. I'm pretty sure that if there's anyone Margaret would want up there, it's you. You're the last person who saw her alive."

"That's why this is so hard to accept." She was crying softly as she spoke. "But you're trying to do too much too soon. Have the assembly today, but make it brief. We need more time to plan the right way to remember Margaret."

After a moment's hesitation, Jaime agreed. He went to work to plan for a brief assembly. Joan began to think about how Pico could celebrate Margaret's life.

The news of her death had spread quickly. There was hardly a sound as students and staff filed into the auditorium later that morning. The mood was somber. Only a few muffled sobs punctuated the heavy silence. Jaime was calm and controlled as he made the brief announcement of Margaret's death.

"She didn't make it: Ms. Juhl is gone."

He informed them when the funeral would be and when visitors could pay their last respects. He also announced that Pico would hold its own memorial assembly the day after the funeral.

"And now," he said, his voice beginning to crack, "let's make the rest of the day just what Ms. Juhl would have wanted it to be—a day when everyone learns. That's the highest tribute we can pay to a teacher we all loved and admired."

Many staff and students sat in silence for a few moments before slowly moving to the aisles. The only noise was the shuffling of feet. The usual din of conversation gradually picked up as people moved back to their classrooms. At the end of the day, several teachers remarked that even though students were subdued, they seemed focused and eager to do their best.

On the day following the funeral service at Largren's Mortuary, Pico held its celebration of Margaret's life. Jaime and members of the Pico Pride Pack had spent hours planning an event that would mirror Margaret's importance to the school. But without her steady hand and unflappable spirit, the planning process had little of the joy and humor always there in the past. Everyone felt her absence, but it spurred them on to work with more intensity and focus than ever before.

Pico's memorial service was comforting, moving, and uplifting for everyone. Before it started, Joan felt almost like an emotional wreck. Yet as she began to speak, the words flowed, steadily, smoothly, and straight from her heart. Only after sitting down did she see the signs of her impact. Staff and students were in tears all over the auditorium. It was then that Joan herself began to feel the full force of what she had said.

As the service drew to a close, Joan's mind wandered back to her first days at Pico and especially to the day that Margaret first came into her classroom, just after Roscoe and Armando had destroyed her day. She beamed through her sadness as she reviewed how far she and the school had come since then. She thought about Roscoe and how well he had been doing in Margaret's class before she died.

Just as she began to wonder how Roscoe would cope with Margaret's loss, she saw him enter the room with Heidi, Armando, and several other students. They were tugging a wagon toward the podium. Perched unsteadily on the wobbly Red Flyer wagon was a large tree, its burlap-wrapped root-ball hanging over the rusted sides. As the ragtag entourage approached the stage with their swaying cargo, Joan's eyes met Roscoe's, and she noticed the tears rolling down one of the largest grins she had ever seen on his face. It was different from the mischievous grin that she had seen so many times in the past. This was the earnest, self-satisfied look of someone who was confident he was doing something really right.

The tree was not in the script, but a smiling nod from Phyllis to Jaime was the only signal he needed to welcome the group and invite them to the stage. To Joan's astonishment, it was Roscoe, not Heidi, who came to the microphone. His words came out in a confident tone.

"Ms. Juhl gone to heaven, but we don't really want to give her up. So us students took our lunch money and bought this here tree. We want you all to come outside and watch as we plant it in front of the school and water it. That way, we can keep Ms. Juhl's spirit with us and remember what she done for us."

Heidi Hernandez followed Roscoe to the microphone and read a poem that she had written. It was about a teacher who planted seeds of learning every day. All the seeds began to grow into beautiful plants, each different from the other. Over the years, so many plants grew that no one could even count them, but everyone could see how much more beautiful the world had become. Joan tried unsuccessfully to hold back the onrush of tears, but gave up as she noticed that she was not alone.

As she left the auditorium, Joan was approached by a man wearing a dark, pinstriped suit that she associated with lawyers, bankers, or diplomats.

"Excuse me," he said. "I'm a former student of Margaret Juhl. She was the best teacher I ever had, and she made a big difference for me. I just wanted to thank you for the eulogy—it meant a lot."

"Margaret meant a lot to me, too," Joan replied. There was something about the stranger that felt very comforting to her, and she wondered who he was. "Have we met before?"

"I don't think so. I'm Steve Riley. I'm a lawyer, and do some work for the school board."

"Of course, Margaret told me about you. She was very proud of you."

"It was herself she should have been proud of. I was a pretty confused and messed up kid when I came into her class. Anyway, thanks again for what you said. Maybe we can get together some time and share reminiscences."

"I'd like that." She hoped he meant it when he promised to call.

━━━━━━━━━━ ❖ ━━━━━━━━━━

"Where did the years go," Jaime Rodriguez asked himself, as he was about to begin his sixth year as Pico's principal. His mind had begun to wander as he sat in the first district principals' meeting of the new school year, half listening to the associate superintendent's sterile review of new district policies. His thoughts floated over Pico's past five years. Being recognized as a school of excellence had been an enormous satisfaction to everyone at the school. But he felt even more gratified at how far he, the staff, and the community had come. Just then, his thoughts were interrupted when the associate superintendent asked, "Why are you smiling? Is there something funny about this sick leave policy?"

"I guess I was admiring all the work you put into it," Jaime responded.

The associate superintendent droned on, and Jaime returned to his memories. This time, he thought about Brenda Connors and what an important force she had been in his career. She had retired and moved to Florida, and Jaime often thought about how much he missed her. If she had been there, he would have expected a note under the table complimenting him on his quick recovery. He thought about how much of her wisdom had been incorporated into his own philosophy.

Just then, his eyes wandered down the table to Sandy Dole, the new principal at Hillview Elementary School, only a few miles from

Pico. She definitely was not smiling. She seemed to be losing a difficult struggle to follow every word in the associate superintendent's presentation. More than anything, she looked plain scared. Was she feeling the same way he had five years ago?

At the end of the meeting, he made a special point of pulling her aside. He introduced himself and asked her, "How's it going?"

She paused, gulped, and stammered, "You want the truth?"

"Nothing but."

"Well," she hesitated, and then plunged ahead. "I'm buried in paper. The school secretary quit two weeks before I started, and we still don't have a replacement. Classes start next week, and I'm short two teachers. I don't know how I'm going to make it."

Jaime felt a wave of nostalgia. Smiling warmly, he said, "That sounds pretty much on target for your first week. I felt the same way my first year at Pico. How about a cup of coffee?"

Two weeks later, Joan Hilliard found herself sitting with a new teacher, Francesca King, on the carved wooden bench under the oak tree casting a shadow on Pico's Margaret Juhl Patio. It was a beautiful September day, and Francesca had asked if they could meet somewhere away from her classroom. Joan automatically suggested the patio—whenever she went there, she felt Margaret's presence.

As Francesca started to talk, it was clear that she had wanted a setting well away from the chaos that had reigned in her classroom that day. When Joan asked, "How's it going?" Francesca's words tumbled out in an almost frantic stream.

"It's going downhill fast. My class is out of control, and I don't know what to do about it. I'm afraid I'm in over my head. Maybe I should quit now before it gets any worse. I've always wanted to be a teacher, but I never thought it could be this tough. I'm working day and night, but I'm still losing my class, and my love life is going to hell. I feel like I'm drowning!"

Joan smiled as memories of her first encounter with Margaret flooded back. "This tree is beautiful, isn't it? It was planted here five years ago in honor of a wonderful teacher, Margaret Juhl. She was my best friend." Joan noticed the puzzled look on Francesca's face and went on. "You're probably wondering what that has to do with you. At about this point in my first year as a teacher, I was ready to quit too."

"That's hard to believe," Francesca protested. "People say you're one of the best teachers here."

"That's where the tree comes in," said Joan with a smile. "I wouldn't have made it through the first term if Margaret Juhl hadn't taken me under her wing. Tell me about your day. If we put our heads together, we might be able to figure out some ways to make it a little easier."

LEADERSHIP LESSONS VII

The Enduring Sequence

Schools, like all organizations, are complex, confusing, and at times, quirky and illusory. Success requires attention to meeting people's needs, producing desired outcomes, dealing with political interests and conflict, and cultivating a shared spirit that imbues work with meaning. Organizations are at once families, factories, jungles, and temples, and effective leaders strive to find a workable balance or equilibrium among the interconnected parts.

Leaders do not accomplish a balance among the values of caring, excellence, justice, and faith by themselves; they seek out others to share the responsibilities. Every leader has a strong suit and an Achilles heel. Good ones play to their strengths and enlist help in areas where they are less effective. Jaime Rodriguez approached his first days thinking about structure and people, relying on his authority and his personality to move the faculty in a new direction. Margaret Juhl relied on her power to counter Jaime's initiative. Later, through his conversations with Brenda, he came to see the limits of his authority and sought out Margaret as an ally. They became a coalition, with Margaret assuming the role of political mediator. Beyond that, with help from Margaret and Brenda, Jaime, Joan, and the Pico Pride Pack began to see the value of ceremony in activating the spiritual aspects of education.

Pico School, like other places of work, has people salted across levels and roles that contribute something special to the harmony of everyday effort. When these people move or retire, they leave lingering traces. That is why Phyllis Gleason's grasp of Pico's history and her flair for shaping the authenticity of key symbolic moments were so vital. The same was true of Bill Hill's role as ambassador to the community and parents. Leaders spot these people and spotlight them for their valued contributions.

As teachers enter the twilight of their days in the classroom, they often try to make sense of their career choice. As they gaze in the rearview mirror, their reflections often capture a dimension of teaching that gets lost in the daily humdrum or swamped by the fault-finding of policy makers and other critics. Through her love of teaching Margaret is leaving a legacy that will inspire others. Her assignment of McCourt's book adds another voice that, at the end of a career, extols the virtues of teaching.

McCourt is right that "it all comes down to you and the kids," and too many teachers have the same experience that he did—the "higher-ups" are too busy with other things to provide help. The consequences are tragic. Administrators feel frustrated and ineffectual, while teachers feel abandoned and alone. School leaders can and should do more. Their highest moral obligation is to nourish the rich legacy, the true values, of teaching. Tracy Kidder agrees:

> Good teachers put snags in the river of children passing by, and over time, they redirect hundreds of lives. . . . There is an innocence that conspires to hold humanity together, and it is made up of people who can never fully know the good they have done. (Kidder, 1989, p. 313)

Each year, thousands of wet-behind-the-ears novices enter the ranks of teaching or educational administration. They have almost no clue about what to expect because they are treading on unfamiliar turf, and everything is a new experience. Their formal preparation has rarely equipped them for the tough reality that lies ahead. Teachers may have learned some of the technical aspects of instruction. Administrators may have mastered some of the skills of managing a school. They typically bring few practical guidelines to their new role beyond their earlier experiences as a student or teacher. There is no other reliable way to make sense of the strange, often incomprehensible, situations that will crop up.

In their insightful book, *The Ropes to Skip and the Ropes to Know*, Ritti and Funkhouser (1987) portray the puzzles of a newcomer muddling through a new assignment and struggling to interpret the elusive subtext or read the mysterious tea leaves everyone else seems to understand:

> Confronted by strange and possibly incomprehensible surroundings, the novice needs an analytical description of what is taking place. In

much the same way as an anthropologist would describe the various functions of ritual, ceremony and law in a strange tribe, or as the travel agent tells the new visitor the do's and don'ts of the local culture, a guide, mentor or seasoned veteran provides the newcomer with some insights into the folkways of his new culture. (p. xix)

Many school districts and schools are trying to help newcomers learn the ropes by assigning mentors to new teachers and principals. Sometimes the formal arrangement works; other times the chemistry is absent. There is an adage, "When you are ready to learn, a teacher will appear." This more natural, serendipitous route brought together Joan with Margaret and Jaime with Brenda. The relationships worked for all parties. The newcomers received wisdom to help guide them through unfamiliar and puzzling challenges. The veterans felt the joy and reward of watching as their "students" profited from their accumulated wisdom.

As the Wizard of Oz said to the Cowardly Lion, "True knowledge comes from experience, and experience you have in plenty." Passing the torch from generation to generation is the primary conduit through which core lessons of leadership are learned. The "school of hard knocks" provides raw material that keeps the accumulated body of key principles current. The teachings of veterans like Margaret and Brenda help novices such as Joan or Jamie mine their firsthand encounters for the nuggets of wisdom that will help them become leaders of a classroom or school. Over time, they acquire seasoned insight and the responsibility to pass along what they have learned. In this traditional rite of passage, past becomes prologue and the beat goes on.

Reflective Questions

1. When you were a newcomer, were you assigned a mentor or coach? If not, did you find one or more colleagues who helped you learn the ropes? How helpful were they?

2. If you are beyond the early stages of your career, how many opportunities do you find to help new colleagues cope with the challenges they face? Do you seek and welcome such opportunities?

EPILOGUE

Before arriving at Pico School, much of what Joan Hilliard and Jaime Rodriguez knew about teaching and the principalship was based on course work, reading, and a few gleanings from earlier experience in the classroom or business world. It was all helpful— anything was better than nothing. But it was only the beginning of their journeys to become effective leaders. Working in the trenches day to day helped each gradually develop know-how and wisdom from experience. While their appreciation for books, and for new ideas and concepts, actually grew over time, they also came to realize that ideas are useful only when harnessed to make things better. The Pico story illustrates the process of converting knowing-about into knowing-how. In the dialogues between Hilliard and seasoned veteran Margaret Juhl and between Rodriguez and his wise mentor Brenda Connors, you witnessed a continuing process of reflection and dialogue about practice. Reflection is something that readers can and should do by themselves, but its value is enhanced immeasurably with help from others—friends, colleagues, and coaches.

A book is only a partial substitute for the kind of sustained, intense, and personal relationship that a young professional can develop with an experienced and wise senior colleague. But we hope that our effort has helped you reap some of the same benefits by raising provocative questions, presenting new perspectives, challenging your thinking, and encouraging your heart. Our fictional characters and events are based on real people or are composites drawn from our own experience as educators and from many practitioners we have encountered along the way. The issues at Pico should be resonant with those you wrestle with today.

We hope our narrative will also prod you to ensure that dialogue and mentoring are a rich and continuing part of your professional life. Both teachers and principals often feel isolated and trapped in their classrooms and offices. Although rarely alone, they are often lonely. They are starved for opportunities to talk freely and openly with other adults who can really understand what their life is like. Too often, outside pressures have sapped the spirit of principals and teachers. A better alternative is for fellow teachers and administrators to become allies and guides for each other. Like Margaret and Joan, Brenda and Jaime, you can help one another create inspiring and elegant conversations. The next step is to apply what you have learned to give new life to classrooms and schools. Preparing the next generation for the future they will inherit is sacred work—nothing is more important. May yours be a soulful journey of joy and reverence.

Annotated Bibliography

A. GENERAL

Bista, M. B., & Glasman, N. S. (1998). Principals' perceptions of their approaches to organizational leadership: Revisiting Bolman and Deal. *Journal of School Leadership, 8*(1), 26–48.

This article combines our four-frame approach to leadership with nine distinct "managerial functions," developing thirty-six different school management strategies. Principals perceived the human resource approach as most extensively used and the political approach as least often used.

Blase, J., & Blase, J. (1997). *The fire is back: Principals sharing school governance.* Thousand Oaks CA: Corwin.

This book examines the concepts of teacher empowerment and shared governance in schools. It shares the experiences of exemplary principals who developed shared governance in their schools, showing how trying to become "one among equals" reenergized principals in their professional work lives.

Bolman, L., & Deal, T. E. (2001). *Leading with soul: An uncommon journey of spirit.* San Francisco: Jossey-Bass.

In Leading With Soul, *we explore the spiritual underpinnings of leadership. We argue that effective leadership ultimately resides in soul and faith and that spirited leaders develop their own gifts so that they may share them with others.*

Bolman, L. G., & Deal, T. E. (2006). *The wizard and the warrior: Leading with passion and power.* San Francisco: Jossey-Bass.

Our research on school leaders consistently finds that their skill in handling the political and symbolic dimensions of their work is vital to their leadership effectiveness. This book focuses on those key leadership capacities.

Bolman, L. G., & Deal, T. E. (2008). *Reframing organizations: Artistry, choice, and leadership* (4th ed.). San Francisco: Jossey-Bass.

This book presents a systematic overview of our ideas about leadership and organizations, with many illustrations and examples from schools, colleges, government, and the private sector.

Conley, S., Gould, J., & Levine, H. (in press). Support personnel in schools: Characteristics and importance. *Journal of Educational Administration.*

An important article highlighting the importance of secretaries, custodians, and other classified workers. A quote in the article from a dissertation (Maxwell, 2004) captures the essence of the authors' argument: "[These individuals are] frequently the glue that holds these school communities together."

Gardner, J. W. (1989). *On leadership.* New York: Free Press.

If you could read only one book on leadership, this would be a very good choice. Gardner packs a lot of wisdom and experience into a highly readable and valuable book.

Johnson, S. M. (1990). *Teachers at work.* New York: Basic Books.

Johnson's book provides a very insightful view of how schools function as workplaces for teachers. She documents many of the barriers and frustrations that teachers encounter in bureaucratic organizations and offers many helpful ideas about how to make schools better places for teaching and learning.

Kidder, T. (1989). *Among schoolchildren.* New York: Houghton Mifflin.

For many years, Kidder has picked subjects to study and present in a detailed nonfiction narrative. His books include House *(1999),* Mountains Beyond Mountains *(2004), and* Strength in What Remains *(2008). In* Among Schoolchildren, *he spotlights Chris*

Zajak, a typical teacher in a conventional New England classroom. He chronicles her triumphs and troubles during the school year and closes with some poetic commentary on the profession of teaching.

Leithwood, K. A. (1990). The principal's role in teacher development. In B. Joyce (Ed.), *Changing school culture through staff development: The 1990 ASCD yearbook*, 71–90. Alexandria, VA: The Association for Supervision and Curriculum Development.

Principals can influence teachers' development of skills, psychological disposition, and "career cycles," Leithwood argues, and this paper outlines some of the ways this can be done.

McCourt, F. (2005). *Teacher man: A memoir*. New York: Scribner.

Frank McCourt taught for thirty years in the New York public schools before beginning a second career as a Pulitzer Prize–winning author. Early in his teaching career, he felt insecure and like a fraud, pretending to be tough and confident when he was not. This book chronicles his journey of self-discovery and professional development.

Palmer, P. (1997). *The courage to teach: Exploring the inner landscape of a teacher's life*. San Francisco: Jossey-Bass.

This book expresses well the belief that teaching has to come from the heart and be rooted in each teacher's identity.

B. POWER AND POLITICS

Kotter, J. P. (1985). *Power and influence: Beyond formal authority*. New York: Free Press.

This book is written for corporate managers, but school leaders will still find it very useful. It provides very clear and comprehensive discussions of power and politics in organizations. Kotter's discussion of the "power gap" in administrative jobs and his chapters on managing your boss are invaluable.

Ritti, R. R., & Funkhouser, G. R. (1987). *The ropes to skip and the ropes to know*. New York: Wiley.

Ritti and Funkhouser's book parallels ours—it's a book designed to help rookies understand the mysteries of management and organization. Their hero is named Stanley instead of Joan or Jaime, and he starts at the bottom of a large, complex corporation.

C. Responding to Human Needs

Barth, R. (1990). *Improving schools from within.* San Francisco: Jossey-Bass.

This is Roland Barth at his best, offering a clear and compelling vision of how principals, teachers, parents, and children can work together to build learning communities.

Kouzes, J. M., & Posner, B. Z. (1988). *The leadership challenge: How to get extraordinary things done in organizations.* San Francisco: Jossey-Bass.

A stimulating and inspiring discussion of the practices of managers operating at their personal best.

Parker, M. T. (1993). *Different approaches to the same challenges: A comparison of U.S. and Japanese principals.* Cambridge, MA: National Center for Educational Leadership.

Based on extensive observations of schools in both Japan and the U.S., Parker points up fascinating contrasts in how principals understand their work and how they are viewed by their constituents.

D. Understanding Structure in Schools

Conley, S., & Enomoto, E. K. (2009). Organizational routines in flux: A case study of change in recording and monitoring student attendance. *Education and Urban Society, 41*(3), 364–386.

This article examines how school administrators changed established "routines" for student attendance—taking in one high school. People often reject efforts to alter routines they are used to; this case study offers insight into how school routines can and do change.

Deal, T. E., Purinton, T., & Waetjen, D. C. (2009). *Making sense of social networks in schools.* Thousand Oaks, CA: Corwin.

Relying on social networks theory, the authors provide a microview of the existing informal structure that governs work-related relationships among principals and teachers.

Meier, D., & Wood, G. (Eds.). (2004). *Many children left behind.* Boston: Beacon House.

This is a collection of essays by some of education's top scholars. Together they laud the intent of the No Child Left Behind (NCLB) legislation, but highlight its many shortcomings. While the law has some structural virtues, these are overshadowed by less obvious flaws.

Mintzberg, H. (1993). *Designing effective organizations: Structure in fives.* New Jersey: Prentice Hall.

Building a structure to fit the demands of work is the cornerstone of organizational design. Mintzberg presents the building blocks of social architecture and develops five models to fit different situations.

Weiss, C., Cambone, J., & Wyeth, A. (1992). Trouble in paradise: Teacher conflicts in shared decision making. *Education Administration Quarterly, 28,* 350–367.

This provocative paper documents many of the promises and pitfalls of shared leadership and teacher empowerment. In a national sample of high schools, Weiss found that there is a price to be paid for participative approaches to decision making, a price about which teachers are often ambivalent. The article suggests that even in progressive schools, teacher leadership is conspicuous mostly for its absence, but we think it also shows how important it is for teachers to become more active leaders.

E. Symbols and Culture in Schools

Bateson, M. C. (1990). *Composing a life.* New York: Penguin Books.

Mary Catherine Bateson, daughter of Gregory Bateson and Ruth Benedict, examines the lives of five prominent women to support her image of life as improvisational art.

Bolman, L. G., & Deal, T. E. (1992, Autumn). What makes a team work? Inside the soul of a new machine. *Organizational Dynamics,* 34–44.

This article uses a famous case of an unusually effective design team to illustrate the symbolic and cultural elements that are critical to peak performance in teams.

Deal, T. E., & Kennedy, A. (1982). *Corporate cultures*. Reading, MA: Addison-Wesley.

A groundbreaking best seller that first popularized the idea of organizational culture. This is the original and still one of the better overviews of what culture is, how it works, and how it can be shaped.

Deal, T. E., & Peterson, K. (2009). *The principal's role in shaping school culture*. Washington, DC: Government Printing Office.

A down-to-earth, practical guide to analyzing and changing school culture.

Deal, T. E., & Redman, P. D. (2009). *Reviving the soul of teaching*. Thousand Oaks, CA: Corwin.

Looks at the historical drift of schools away from spiritual roots toward technical standards. Highlights the contemporary need for a better balance between magic and metrics.

F. Ethics in Teaching and Leading

Bolman, L. G., & Deal, T. E. (1992). Images of leadership. *The American School Board Journal, 179*(4), 36–39.

This article spells out the four values of excellence, caring, justice, and faith that are discussed in Chapters 11 and 12, and relates them to four different images of a school: family, factory, jungle, and cathedral.